ELECTRONIC KNITTING

an introduction for Brother and Knitmaster Knitters

KATHLEEN KINDER

Photography: George Kinder

J.W.Lambert & Sons

Kathleen Kinder The Dalesknit Centre Settle

North Yorkshire BD24 9BX Tel.(07292) 2809

ISBN 0 9506668 6 6

£6.95

Other books by Kathleen Kinder

A Resource Book for Machine Knitters	1979
A Second Resource Book for Machine Knitters	1980
The Passap Duomatic, Deco and Forma	1981
A Resource Book Pattern Supplement	1983
The Machine Knitter's Book of the Ribber Vol.1	1984
Techniques in Machine Knitting (B.T.Batsford)	1983

Text prepared by George Kinder

on a micro-computer with word-processor

Printed by J. W. Lambert & Sons, Station Road, Settle, N. Yorks.

CONTENTS

Photos, Diagrams and Patterns.

ELECTRONIC KNITTING

an introduction for Brother and Knitmaster Knitters

Foreword

This publication came about partly because knitters requested it. I have temporarily set aside other work in order to tackle what has become a pressing matter. It all started as the result of 19 questions and comments sent to me by Mrs Gilpin and the Wallsend Knitting Club, and continued with letters, phone conversations and discussions with various knitters in the Dalesknit Centre.

Though there are books from overseas which deal with different aspects of electronic knitting on one or other machine, there is very little literature which serves as a general introduction and a guide to some of the problem areas of the subject. I hope therefore that both knitters and dealers will find this little book useful. Perhaps it may also persuade some non-electronic knitters to join the ranks of those who own these remarkable machines. The book is, after all, just a beginning, and a small contribution to help open up a very large and fascinating subject, both for users of electronic machines and interested enquirers.

Note on the contents

Although there is some advice here on work with ribbers, I have concentrated on single bed knitting, because help on double bed knitting will be given in more detail in the forthcoming work "The Machine Knitter's Book of the Ribber. Vol 2" The day is not far off when electronic knitters will be able to have a full scale, concentrated work devoted solely to their needs and interests.

I welcome comments from knitters both with regard to this book and with regard to what they want future publications to contain for electronic knitting. Are patterns written out in full in six sizes still in demand? If so,please consider the expense of a small print run and the amount of space both you and I will be paying for, one sixth of which only can be of limited value to you. All Knitmaster 500-60 knitters have a Knitradar. How many Brother 910 knitters have the Knitleader? Would knitters accept charting device diagrams with explanations of techniques and shaping breakdowns given in one size? Thank you in anticipation for your help.

* Brother 910 MK II. Please read the notes at the end of the book (pp.98,103,107)

From Punchcard to Electronic

The current interest in home computers may have something to do with the growing popularity of electronic knitting machines, but a more important reason is the recognition of the tremendous creative potential of these machines. There is also an increase in electronic knitting machine ownership amongst new knitters, but even they, like those who have had other machines, must live for the moment within the limits set by the punchcard. Many knitters feel inhibited by this, and wonder why they bothered to go electronic. Others, like Passap knitters before them, feel left out in clubs and classes when everything is geared to the punchcard machine. At least, that is how it appears at present. For how long remains to be seen, but knitters with electronic machines will be in an advantageous position as the market moves towards more versatile systems.

For the moment, electronic knitters are the pioneers, and an age of discovery is always a time of great excitement, interest and enjoyment even though there are moments of frustration.

Punchcard repeats.

It is, however, worth pointing out that the 24 and 40 stitch repeat systems (40 for the Passap Deco) are two of the most valuable repeat systems there are. The more one explores other repeat systems, the more one is forced back to the multiples of 24 and 40. Both have 6 factors or multiples which offer repeats within the large repeat.

Repeat system	Multiples or factors
24	2,4,8, 3, 6,12
40	2,4,8, 5,10,20

For instance, take 30. Its factors are 2,3,6,5,10,15, of which only 15 is not included in those for 24 or 40.

We should not resent the familiar, but we should use it from choice, not because we have to. The 60 stitch repeat system has even more potential. It offers 59 different bases, each with its own multiples or factors. It offers more interesting pattern delineations, arrangements and partnerships within a pattern sequence for stitches like tuck, slip and lace as well as for Fair Isle.Motif knitting and its relationship to garment shape present a whole new field to be explored. The Fibre-Artist Knitter has the larger repeats to go at for hangings, furnishings and pictorial effects on sweaters. There is also much greater scope for the jacquards and Aran tucks, double bed as well as single (as I am discovering). Features like pleats involving lace, cables, embossed jacquard, tuck and slip stitches can be arranged exactly to suit without having to worry about their not fitting into a 24st repeat.

As always, freedom implies discipline and the use of a variety of human skills not normally associated with knitting IF we are to enjoy even a small part of the riches at our fingertips.

Notes on Passap and Deco Patterning

a. Fair Isle - can be copied as it is on the Deco card, if the repeat covers the whole width of the card. If the pattern can be broken down into smaller repeats, then one complete repeat only is necessary. **Note.** If the second repeat is offset, then two motifs make up one complete repeat, the one staggered in the space above the other.

If we use single bed Fair Isle, then the height of the design will be more compressed than that produced by the Passap bird's eye jacquard setting.

b. Tuck and Slip. The Deco card selector can repeat rows of pattern twice or four times (2 or 4 on the dial).As an electronic knitter, you can decide how to mark for a 1,2,3 or 4 row tuck or slip. With a fine yarn and a tuck lace you could go to 6. On the Deco card, the holes represent the needles which tuck and slip. It is the pattern shape or delineation which is of most value to you. (For help on understanding Passap terms see A Resource Book for Machine Knitters and The Machine Knitter's Book of the Ribber. Vol.1).

For Brother 910 owners. Knitleader or Ribber?

As an author on the ribber, I offer strange advice. If you have to make a choice, go for the Knitleader first. The full size Knitleader is a boon to the 910 owner. It is a good idea to support the Knitleader on a block of wood or polystyrene. The plastic cover on the back of some early 910 models had a tendency to pull away under the weight of the Knitleader. The back on the newer models is reinforced. Even so, a support is a safeguard, provided it does not shore up the Knitleader above the level of the machine top.

For Knitleader and Knitradar owners

At the time of writing, the majority of available garment patterns are for the punchcard machines, though Knitmaster's Modern Knitting and Brother Fashion are including more for their electronics. You will also find patterns, hints and tips in my own publications and also in magazines like Knitting Machine Digest, Machine Knitting News and The Australian Machine Knitters magazine. The three magazines have regular book reviews on what's new in the machine knitting scene, and electronic knitting is bound to feature in more new publications.

a. Patterns, to a charting device knitter, are means of inspiration and sources of technical methods to use in one's own knitting. A charting device knitter needs a collection of sizes in the three main pattern blocks (see my Resource Book Pattern Supplement) from which to design garment shapes. Once you are a charting device user, the pattern potential of the electronic machine can begin to be tapped. Every stitch pattern has its own stitch and row tension, and repeats outside the 24 limit could produce stitch and row tensions which are quite unfamiliar.A charting device then is an essential aid.

b. A new freedom offered by the electronics is the facility to plan motifs and panels, vertical and diagonal, anywhere within the same horizontal limits, but you cannot introduce another motif halfway up the knitting of another unless it is marked on the card and is included as part of the first motif. The full size, full scale Knitleader is a great boon here. Selective pattern placement has great possiblities for both the Fashion and Craft knitting trades. Having colour knitting controlled and directed within a certain area can be more acceptable, and indeed have more impact, than overall multicolour patterning.

Planning motifs and sprays of connected shapes along invisible diagonal lines is an artistic technique for which the Japanese have been famous for centuries, as their Kimonos, Kesode and No robes reveal so splendidly. This traditional expertise is being used to great effect on knitwear by means of the electronic machines.

Planning Motifs on the Charting Device

How do we plan diagonal motifs on the Knitradar?

First, take a piece of greaseproof paper. Fold it down the middle (at line 0) for speed and draw the quarter size half scale block.(Note: quarter size is half of a half. see fig.2). Cut round the lines and open out (Fig.1). Your tension swatch should include a motif. Measure across with a triangular scale or metric ruler and halve the amount. Measure the length in the same way. Use these two measurements to plot the position of the motifs across the opened out piece, using the two arms of a cross symbol to represent the widest horizontal and longest vertical measurements of the motif. Draw a rough shape of the motif round the cross marks, taking care not to wander outside the limits set by the arms of the cross. It is a good idea to draw the motifs left of 0 in a different colour from those on the right. Now, fold the greaseproof block in half and transfer the motif marks to the half scale, quarter size Knitradar sheet, using a different colour for those which relate to the LEFT side of 0 (dotted in Fig.2). Make a note of the colours you've used for each side.

Programming the machine.

Before you begin, set the width indicator for the correct number of stitches, remembering to include any stitches in the main colour as separating stitches if two or more motifs are to be placed side by side.

For the rest, you can program as you knit at the point where the vertical point of the motif on the Knitradar sheet strikes the stitch ruler. Make a note of the row and the placement of the N.1. cam and the points cams. Make quite sure you have the direction in which the motif is facing correctly programmed. On a symmetrical motif, it won't matter,so have No.2 left hand light on.

Regine Faust suggests that you cut out paper shapes of your motif and arrange them to your liking on a basic sweater shape first. (see book list) You could certainly do that before following the instructions above for the Knitradar.

The Knitleader

The principles outlined above for the Knitradar can be applied when you want to use a quarter size block (Fig.2). Remember you work to full scale and your motifs and sketch marks are full size measured directly off the tension swatch. The best tool to use on unlined greaseproof is the L-shaped triangular scale (Brother), as its transparent surface is marked in square cms. The smaller, white triangular scale is better for the Knitradar as two of its sides are marked for the half scale situation. Be careful on unlined paper. Draw a line at right angles to another ONLY by using the right angle of the scale as a guide.

Programming for Brother knitters.

Again, the information given for Knitmaster is useful, but you will need the linear measurements given by the arms of the cross (one per motif) in order to plot the positions. Please note, the first needle position is determined by the **widest part** of the motif, which could be at least halfway up. That is why the cross symbol is so useful. Using the pattern switch in the up position is easiest for beginners. When you are more confident you use the middle switch for A and B motifs adding another motif alongside the first. (see later section)

PENS, PENCILS AND RUBBERS.

In the original equipment of both the Brother 910 and the Knitmaster 500-560, pencils were provided. They still are with the Knitmaster machines, but Brother have replaced the black and red pencils and the ink rubber that accompanied them with a non-fillable, black, oil-based, fibre-tipped pen and a grey, pencil-type ink rubber. Dissatisfaction was expressed with the pencils for both makes of machine, because the pencil marks wore off the sheet after repeated use, and therefore the pattern became inaccurate.

There are certain situations where pencils are invaluable (for one-offs especially). Brother knitters who want to make the most of their mylar sheets should acquire these pencils from their dealer. Knitmaster writing equipment will not work on the Brother machine, and vice versa. The long, grey pencil rubber is all-purpose and is ideal for removing isolated spots on both Brother and Knitmaster mylar sheets. It is available from dealers and newsagents. An ink rubber can be used over large surfaces to clean up the diluted mess left by a solvent. Dry it off first with a clean cloth before using the rubber. NOTE. Most of the pens are fibre-tipped (you can get refill tips for the Brother pen)and their flow is controlled by pressure. Shake the pen first to get the flow going and then use lightly and firmly on the sheet. Too much pressure means too much flow and then blots drop onto the pattern.

Don't over-sharpen the pencils. A too-sharp point can pierce the sheet. In fact, it is probably better to sharpen with a knife. Always mark the sheets on a firm, smooth surface. A pitted table top is the last thing to use in these circumstances. Even if you don't pierce the sheet, the pencil or tool could form a depression and not a mark, and a mispattern will occur.

BROTHER 910

a) Pencils provided or bought additionally.

The red pencil is the heavier of the two and is suitable to use over large surfaces. Rub out with the rubber provided or with an ink rubber.

Either pencil is ideal for use on one of the existing sheets where you are inserting a design into a corner or small space and intend to use it for a one-off. I have tuck patterns in various empty spaces on the pattern sheets. Use the pencil on an area where you have used solvents and where you suspect the solvents are beginning to destroy the surface of the sheet. There is no evidence yet that they do, but there are warnings on most solvent bottles that the solvent could destroy certain plastics, so forewarned is forearmed.

b) The pen provided or bought additionally

The surface the pen gives is matt and its ink velvety, dense black in colour. It is particularly good for large areas. Use the template to ensure the ink doesn't run over into adjacent empty squares. Though most British machine knitters seem to like the pen, Japanese and Australian knitters, who have used the pen for some time are more critical. Its ink flow can be erratic and unreliable, especially towards the end of its life.

c) The Edding 1800 Profipen 0.5(obtainable from good stationers)

This is cheaper than the recommended Brother pen, its nib is much finer, it requires less pressure and it produces a shiny surface like most drawing inks. Since light-blocking is an essential feature of the pattern making process on the 910, it follows that there must be several drawing and printing inks which can be used successfully (though knitters report varying success with Rotring ink). I prefer the Edding to the recommended Brother pen, especially for the finer work, but I have used both successfully in the one design, the Edding for the outline and the Brother pen for the filling in. Though matt over shine and dense black over grey-black look rather strange together,the machine responded as it was meant to do. Moreover, both pens can be used to give contrast in, say, a woven lace or tuck and lace pattern as marked on the card.

d) Staedtler Marsmatic M 150.

This is a pen used with the ink, Staedtler Marsmatic 747 T.9. The nibs to use are M 1.0, M 0.7, M 0.5. The price of the pen is around £5.00. You remove the ink from the cards by the use of a **wet** plastic rubber. I am grateful to Mrs.Anne Wells of Gillingham for writing to me with the information. Mrs Wells also adds that a Black Prince pencil (cost 20p.) works on the Knitmaster 500-560, but of course the pens recommended above are for the Brother alone.

Note 1. The advantage of ink is that one can use a brush for large areas to be blocked in. It is quicker to use a paint brush than a pen. It is important to buy a good quality artist's brush.

Note 2. If your 910 has any difficulty picking up the marks from any of the pens and pencils discussed above in a)b)c)and d)consult your dealer. It may be that one works and the other doesn't, or there could be a voltage problem in the electrical supply to your machine, or the machine's response could be below par.

Note 3. Some knitters report that the black pen supplied with the Knitleader also works well on the mylar sheet.Marks can be wiped off with a damp cloth.

Note 4. Highly recommended is Higgins Black Magic waterproof drawing ink, No.4465.

Knitmaster 500-560

a)Pencils provided.

One is finer than the other.I prefer to use these pencils for most of the patterns, since I am unlikely to be involved in long production runs. Pencils are also good to use when one wishes to select portions of designs on the pre-marked cards provided with the machine, or when one wishes to alter the card return direction. Blot out the existing marks in the right hand columns with blobs of self-adhesive paper which are easily removed later. The pre-marked cards are made of a soft paperlike substance. Do not apply any harsh solvents and use only a soft pencil rubber on the surface of the pre-marked cards. The blank mylar sheets are made of tougher plastic.

b)The Pilot Super-colour Silver pen (Extrafine)

This is a non-refillable pen containing permanent-type ink, silver in colour. It provides permanent marks on the mylar sheets. It is excellent for large surface coverage but it can flood if too much pressure is used.A dot is sufficient for isolated stitches, but do be careful the ink doesn't run across blank squares. The disadvantage is that silver doesn't show up very well on the transparent sheet.

c) The Original Outliner-fine point

These pens are made by Sakura, Japan, and are available in at least 6 colours from most newsagents. The price of each pen is about a third less than that of the Pilot pen. These outliners are a great boon to Knitmaster knitters. Basically, each pen is silver but as one marks, the colour forms the outline edge and then runs across. A dot will suffice for one stitch. If one buys a selection of colours then one's design can be coloured on the sheet for easy colour reference. Moreover, these metallic colours are much better to see than plain silver. I also find that the colour edge inhibits the flow and this is a decided advantage. Pencil, Pilot silver and Sakura outliners can be used on the same design. There may well be outliners produced by other firms which will also work on the Knitmaster mylar cards.

SOLVENTS FOR THE PENS

Liquid-paper thinner or similar, applied to the sheet will remove the ink from the pens recommended for both Brother and Knitmaster machines. Use a cloth to mop up the diluted ink mess and follow by cleaning with the grey pencil rubber or ink rubber. The Edding pen left the most marks, but the rubber removed them instantly.

However, an accident with the green Outliner reminded me of the Chinese story of Burnt Pig. It is very easy to unscrew the main part of the pen so that the ink floods all over one's hands. This is what I did. The ink dropped onto a blank mylar sheet. I hastily seized a bottle of surgical spirit to clean my hands. The surgical spirit splashed onto the mylar sheet and dissolved the ink. Later, I tried it on both Brother and Knitmaster mylar sheets in more controlled conditions,to find that surgical spirit was just as effective as expensive solvent. In the story, the Chinese boy burnt down a house everytime he wanted roast pig. In future, I do not intend either to buy expensive solvent or to waste half a bottle of surgical spirit everytime I want to erase a mark.Warning.Surgical spirit has certain destructive properties and it should be used with care. Do not leave the bottle within the reach of children.

Ordinary Pencil

Use ordinary pencil on the mylar sheet when you want to convey messages to yourself, but not to the machine. For example, Brother knitters will need another L window when they put a lace pattern beside one whose marks already occupy the existing L window. Leave room for the new L window in the sheet.

A Magnifying Glass

This is invaluable whether you have poor eyesight or not. You can buy a magnifying glass (9cm diameter) with a handle,from chemists or from a good photographic supply shop. The glass with a stand or with a neck strap is the most useful, but tends to cost quite a bit more than the basic glass with handle. If you are handy with gadgets or know someone who is, then it would be cheaper to construct your own support. It is obviously much better to work on the mylar sheet with both hands free.

Are Knitmaster and Brother blank mylar sheets interchangeable?

When you place the one over the other the perforations seem to be exactly the same. The card plastic is very similar, though the Knitmaster has a less shiny surface. The markings, however, are completely different and the Knitmaster card is 1cm shorter. If, in an emergency, you have to use a card from the other make, you will need to transpose all the essential lines. The best way to find out what you need is to place a blank card for your machine over one from the other and decide what additional lines like the set line, L window or buzzer column (Knitmaster) you need to pencil in. Note: The first row on the Brother card is 14 clear rows down and on the Knitmaster 10 clear rows down in the machine.

Can I use patterns on the pre-marked cards from other makes of machines?

The answer is:"Yes". With the exception of lace, all the pattern mark symbols are the same. The program instructions will be different, of course. With lace, concentrate on using fashioned lace patterns from the other system. Knitmaster, you begin with two knit rows, and Brother, you end with them. The transfer pattern marks are the same, but Knitmaster owners need to mark shunting sequences at the right, and Brother knitters the stocking stitch rows in the L window at the left.

CLEANING THE MACHINE

Always keep the machine covered when it is not in use and keep it away from direct sunlight which can disrupt the electronics. If you haven't got one of the specially-made machine covers, then cover the machine with a piece of polythene sheet and an attractive cloth. Do not cover with a cloth only as dust will go through. Keep the machine itself clean with surgical spirit, but keep surgical spirit away from painted letters and figures. It could remove them. Wipe off all dirty oil and oil that has gone yellow and waxy. Extend the needles to H.P. and wipe above and below with a clean cloth moistened with surgical spirit. Every few months, remove all the needles from the bed and clean them with a cloth moistened with surgical spirit. When the bed is empty of needles, take a hand-held vacuum over the needle grooves and suck out all the dust and fluff. Do not use a blower, and please see that all needle cams and double-eyed bodkins are out of reach of the vacuum. It is a good idea to use a vacuum regularly when all the needles are in the bed, as an electronic machine tends to attract more dust than a punchcard one does. **Never** dismantle an electronic machine to investigate its inner workings. That is a job for a qualified electronic engineer.

How do I know when to take the needles out for their spring-clean?

When the needles are in A position their latch tips lie just outside the rectangular slots of the metal bed. If the slots are edged with grime that you can't clean off easily with the needles in place, and if the needle stems themselves can be only partially cleaned, then it is time for the big removal and clean up. Actually, if you keep up with regular cleaning sessions, it may not be necessary to remove the needles at all. **Note.** Surgical spirit is not freely available in the U.S.A. Untreated alcohol or other spirit cleaners may be suitable. Consult your dealer.

Cleaning and oiling the carriages.

Slide them from the bed. Clean off all the old oil and fluff underneath using a soft brush or cotton bud. Clean with spirit and re-oil lightly, using a bottle with a brush in the neck for a controlled flow. Clean all the rails and all moving metal parts and then re-oil. Remove the needle marking strip and clean with a cloth. Slide it under the needles and see that it is correctly placed. This is particularly important for the Brother. Green 1 must be at 1 on the right of 0, so see that the last orange and green marks are placed at 100, left and right respectively. Put the 910 carriage on the lace rail and insert the tooth-pick end of the crochet tool into the Brother timing belt. With a clean cloth moistened with surgical spirit, pull the belt out and round. You'll be surprised at the amount of dirt on the cloth. Now do the same with a clean cloth moistened with oil. You'll find you have considerably reduced the noise the belt makes.

Don't forget to clean the lace carriages.

They need attention too. Check the little square magnet is still in place on the back of the Brother lace carriage and always keep the spare Knitmaster carriage in the box provided.

Do not leave cards in the machine when you have finished with them. Do not handle them with oily hands. Brush the cards with a pad or cloth before putting them in the machine or back in the plastic wallet. At the end of a knitting session, put the inspection button on and take the curl cord out of the Knitmaster carriage. Then switch off. When you return, switch on, replace the cord, take the memory and switch off the inspection button. On the Brother, always leave the carriages outside the orange marks. Do the same when you input a new program. The lace carriage can be left on the rail at the end of a knitting session. Close the lid on the Brother pattern panel. This lid is rather fragile, so treat it with respect and do not bend it back.

Knitmaster 500-560

Your system is very easy to manipulate and very easy to follow, but first have you set up the machine in the order given in the manual p19ff? Knitters have complained about the machine behaving oddly, but usually, if it does, it is because the instructions in the manual have not been followed. For example, they forget initially to plug the curl cord into the carriage (usually the lace carriage).The machine should be set up ready before it is switched on. If you are doing only stocking stitch, then switch off the power, remove the curl cord, the N.1. cam and the card from the machine.

The points cams, the Needle One cam (N.1.cam) and No.2 button.

The points cams.

These set the limits on the pattern. Outside of them, the pattern will knit stocking stitch on the Fair Isle, weaving and lace settings, but will loop on tuck and slip on slip if the No.1 button left hand light is on. For slip and tuck with the No.1 button right hand light on, the stitches outside the PCs will knit. You must pass the PCs with the carriage or else there will be a mispattern. Similarly, if you hesitate for more than 30 seconds in the middle of the knitting and the carriage is stationary, then there will also be a mispattern.

When you decrease, you move the points cams opposite to the decrease **first**, because the memory for the points cam nearest to the carriage is ready to be acted upon.**Don't** forget to keep an eye on the Knitradar and anticipate any increases or decreases. Have the points cams just inside the edge of the knitting - a couple of stitches are usual. On a jacquard jacket you can include the band as you knit simply by moving the points cam in 13 -18 sts or so. A plain area is knitted at the side of the pattern, and your band is incorporated in the front.

The Needle One cam.

The Needle One cam decides the starting and finishing points of the pattern as indicated on the width indicator below the pattern card and No.1 grid (extreme left) on the pattern card itself. Usually, we place the N.1. cam (with the red line towards us) in the middle of the bed unless we are motif knitting or want an odd number of pattern repeats. In the latter case, we place the N.1. cam **half a pattern** width to the right or left of 0. If you are a beginner, it is easier to start with the N.1. cam in the middle. Why? The answer is that if it is eventually outside of the W.P. needles, we must still pass it with the carriage. It is the brain behind the pattern placement and must be included in every pattern operation that involves increases and decreases. You can indeed do without the N.1. cam. The pattern is then controlled by the left hand points cam and the pattern begins from there. As soon as you move the points cams, the pattern is disrupted. Therefore always get into the habit of using the N.1. cam.

What do I do with the N.1. cam, when I'm shaping a round neck (not lace)?

During the knitting of, first the right side and then the left side of the neck, the N.1. cam will be isolated in the middle. Leave the points cam positioned over it. Do not move the P.C. in this situation. You can easily cope with neatening the neck edges as you decrease by pushing the edge needles to D position and setting the cams to knit back. Providing the carriage passes both the P.C. and the N.1. cam, the pattern will be correct.

Neck shaping in lace.(N.1. cam in centre as above)

First wind off enough spare yarn to cast off the neck side stitches. You will have to move in the P.C. when the carriage is at the opposite side. Decrease with the spare yarn at the same time. Move the P.C. two sts in from the edge to stop the lace carriage forming a hole at the edge. The N.1. cam is now beyond the P.C. limits. The pattern will be correct if the carriage passes over the N.1. cam on every row. Use this method also when the N.1. cam is placed other than centrally.

The direction light (No.2).

This is the third feature which, taken in conjunction with the P.Cs. and the N.1. cam determines correct patterning. No.2 button determines the direction of the pattern, its starting and finishing points from the N.1. cam as focal point. The best way to explain is by the diagram which Doris Coutts has used so helpfully in several publications and articles.

When the left light is on.

The pattern begins with the first stitch to the **left** of the N.1. cam, and ends with the first stitch at the **right.** We take 24 as the pattern width.

Pattern width indicator

1 ———————— 24

N.1.C.

24 ———————— 1'24 ———————— 1

When the right light is on

The pattern begins with the first stitch to the **right** of the N.1.C. and ends with the first stitch to the **left.**

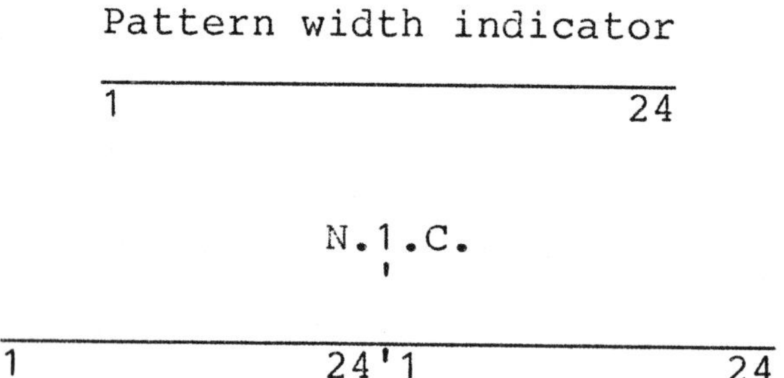

Two catch phrases to learn

Left is left for stitch and light
Right is right for stitch and light

The image on the pattern sheet

When we have the left light on, the image on the pattern sheet is reversed on the purl side of the knitting, but on the knit side, it is the same as that on the pattern sheet.

When we have the right light on, the image on the pattern sheet is the same as that which appears on the purl side of the knitting (lace is a good example). On the knit side, the image is the reverse of what is on the pattern sheet.

The left light is used more often than the right. If we switch between lights, there can be occasional pattern disruption (see mirror image), so it is important to memorize the new position four times with the carriage, or we can switch the machine off and on again before we re-program.

The patterns and the lights

In the manual, most of the patterns employ the second button LH light setting. The exceptions are lace and motifs in tuck and slip. If one uses the LH light in lace, then faggot lace will become the heavier eyelet lace and vice versa, because one has altered the relationship between the lie of the pattern, the selected needle and the direction of the lace carriage.

If one is doing, say, one or two panels of tuck lace or motif tuck, then there is a good case for using the RH light, so that one will see on the purl side the exact image of the pattern (p.115 of the manual).

Note: When the N.1.cam is moved within a motif area, it appears to alter the direction of the pattern. It seems so because the N.1. cam carries the first and last needle positions with it. In actual fact, only No.2 light alters direction.

How do I interpret punchcard patterns?

One could also add, Brother 910 patterns, because the problem is the same. There are two aspects:-

1. The punchcard pattern is centred on 0 in the needlebed, and the 910 with all buttons down for overall patterning centres its pattern on green No.1.(the same thing).

The image on the punchcard and on the 910 sheet (using the setup above) is in reverse to what appears on the knit side of the fabric. This matters to the 500-560 owner only when the pattern follows a strong directional line. To cope with both aspects of the problem:-

1. Place the N.1.C. half the pattern width (i.e. between the 12th and 13th stitches in the case of a punchcard pattern) to the left or right of 0 on the bed.
2. Use the second button,RH light.

The problem of tuck and slip

The electronic machines (Knitmaster and Brother) have a great advantage over the punchcard machines in that one only needs to mark the stitch to be tucked or slipped. A reversal is necessary and this is provided on the 500-560 by the No.1 button, right hand light on (Brother 910 No.6. button up). On the punchcard you translate the blanks as pattern marks and not the holes.

Tuck and slip are usually purlside rightside patterns and to avoid confusion myself, I have taken to having No.2. button RH light on, so that I copy exactly what is on the punchcard, and know that providing I begin the pattern with the N.1.C. placed between the 12th and 13th stitch to the left (better left than right, because of isolation during neck shaping) I shall get what I see on the punchcard on the purlside of the fabric. 0 on the bed is now the same as that on the punchcard machine.

This solution, of course, is only temporary and applies to the above situation. Once one understands the system, one should be able to move between lights and shift the N.1.C. as well.

If you have the N.1.C. in the centre and Button 2 left hand light on, then the first stitch is to the left of 0, and the tuck or slip stitch is worked in the opposite direction from that on the punchcard. The centre of the punchcard will again be between the 12th and 13th needle to the left or right of 0.

Knitmaster Card 3 - tuck lace and tuck rib

Garment patterns in tuck featuring Knitmaster Card 3 and Toyota Card 3 are very popular. Please note - Knitmaster Card 3 and Toyota Card 3 are the same card, but the Toyota card needs to be used upside down to produce the same patterning groups as Knitmaster Card 3A. Unfortunately, the layout on the 500-560 card for 1 (3) is different again. This is just one problem one can get with relating a punchcard translation to an electronic card. It is far better to understand how the system works and then one can arrange needle groups for tuck lace and tuck rib to suit oneself. Brother 910 owners: the principle is the same for you. Use KCII and No.6 button up.

Note on Card 1 (3)

There is a mistake on p.9 of the 560 Pattern book relating to the needle setups for Card 1 (3). What has probably happened is that the punchcard setups have been reproduced unthinkingly. Compare with the correct setups on p.27 of the manual. Now is as good a time as any to understand the system. Take No.1 sheet out of your pack and look at pattern 3. To find which needles you can place in N.W.P. (or on the ribber for rib tuck), you are interested in empty vertical spaces which are empty for the **complete** length of the pattern. In order to relate the setup to the pattern card we have the right light on and the N.1.C. in the centre. No.2 square will do as a starter. The pattern groups are in 3s with the needle tucking first on one side of the group and then on the other, so if we put the 2nd needle to NWP then the 6th also goes to NWP on the right of 0 in the bed. The needle setup will look like this. * = tucking needle.

a) for the first sequence

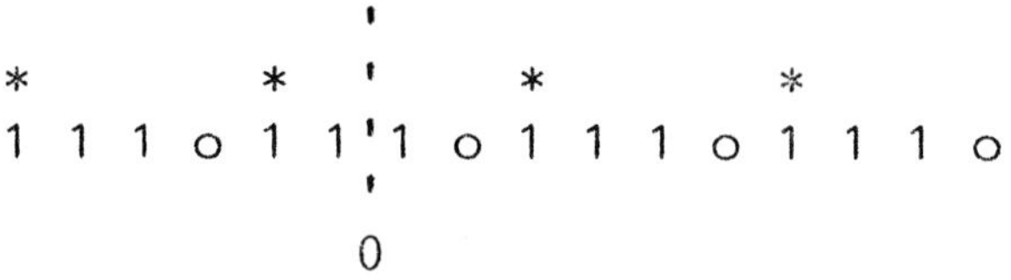

b) for the second sequence

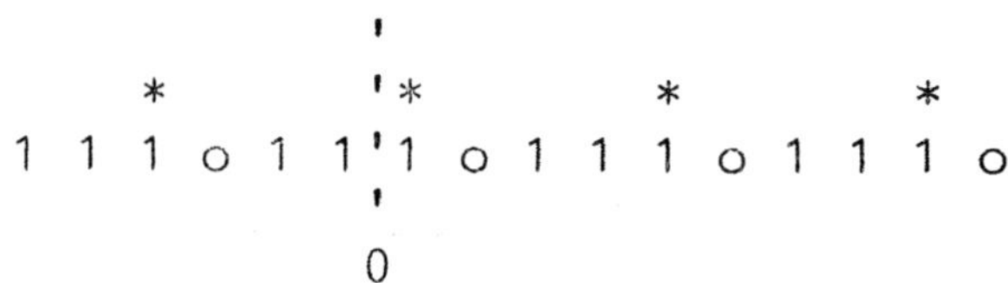

Another setup is possible. Can you work it out? (Start with needle 4)

Brother 910 owners-the pattern under discussion can be produced by the one placed bottom left under the label "Tuck and slip patterns" on the mylar sheet featuring Knitmaster lace meshes. It is easier for Brother 910 knitters to program an overall pattern on the top setting of the pattern selector choosing G1 as your FNP.

Tuck lace makes very attractive panels providing there are not too many tuck loops held at once by the needle. Too many produce distortion in the stocking stitch fabric on each side of the panel.

Long vertical blanks on the punchcard

Sometimes for speed, a pattern designer will leave long vertical blanks on the punchcard to indicate main bed needles in NWP or WP needles on the ribber. Do not be deceived by these. The empty columns do not represent tuck stitches, which must alternate in pattern groups of holes and blanks going up the card. Instead, put the needles represented by these blank columns in NWP on the main bed, and work out the punchcard pattern with the right light on, N.1.C. between the 12th and 13th stitch right or left of 0. Start your setup from this point so that 0 on the bed equals 0 on the punchcard. Though you need to mark out only one pattern repeat, it is wise in the case of punchcard patterns to mark out for 24 sts. as per your Pattern sheet 1, at least until you understand what you are doing.

You can always check by taking the brush assembly off the front of the carriage. Put the cam lever to slip (the patterning needles are easy to see), button 1, right hand light on, and move the carriage across. You will see the needles which slip stay at B, and the other knitting needles will come out to C.

Other points

1) When a tuck pattern incorporates stocking stitch rows, these are indicated by blanks on the card. Do not forget to include the last two rows of a pattern; they are easily forgotten.

2) To repeat a row- put on the inspection button and the last row of the pattern will be repeated. This is especially good for tuck lace where you need so many rows tuck, so many rows stocking stitch, or, for the tea-cosy pattern (8 rs slip, 2 rs stocking stitch, Card 1(1)).

3) The use of double length (3) and double width (4) buttons- Please note that the double length - elongation process takes place from the right on the 500-560 machine. Therefore one cannot use the colour changer to co-ordinate with pattern marks since the exchange of yarn must be done at the right for the design to be correct. One can use e.o.n. tucks and F.I. with double width button , and course, one must take account of the double width in one's needle

allocation for patterns on the bed (especially important for the 910).

When you make mistakes when you are using No. 3 button, pull back to the right hand side. If you want to use the colour changer on elongated, multi-coloured tucks, jacquards and slips, then it is best to mark out the pattern in double length and not use the No.3 button at all. In any case it cannot be used on the jacquard setting.

4) There is no setting for both ways free move slip on the 560 carriage. It is best to program two blank rows a few stitches wide on the card if you need this setting. You could make a point of marking for free moves on every available card. It is also useful to have a program for fishermans rib marked on the card, one row blank and one row blacked in (ie the opposite way to the carriage setting).

Reasons: On the main carriage:-

Cam lever on C- knits from right to left, slips from left to right.

Cam lever on E- knits from right to left, tucks from left to right.

5) To use the ribber transfer carriage (RT1), remove the points cams and N.1.C. outside the range covered by the transfer.

6) Put the inspection button on at the end of a knitting session. When you return and have prepared to pattern knit again, press the release lever. The main body of the carriage springs up. Take it across the bed four times to re-program before you press the top down. Push off the inspection button and knit.

The Three Methods of Automatic Card Return

Two of these methods are on p.115 of the manual. Most Knitmaster knitters seem to be unaware of the possibilities offered by the three methods and we give one or two options in this book, just to set you going. The three methods are marked on the pattern sheet featuring the half star.

1) The standard method is marked on the majority of cards. At the top of the pattern a mark in the buzzer column ensures that it speaks, and the card returns quickly to the first row.

2) Card 1(1) is marked differently. Try it and see. The downward column is marked, but the card is fed upwards, a row at a time, to the bottom, where it resumes normal motion. The top row is knitted only once, so this method is ideal to knit a completely symmetrical motif from only half the pattern. The direction arrow is the guide for when you go wrong. It shows you which way to turn the card, back or forward when you have pulled back. There is no buzzer and no quick return.

3) The third method was contributed to the To and Fro Electronic Mini-club Newsletter by Mike Eaton. It is as follows:- You mark columns one and two as per second method,

Half Shetland Star (3 positions) 500-560

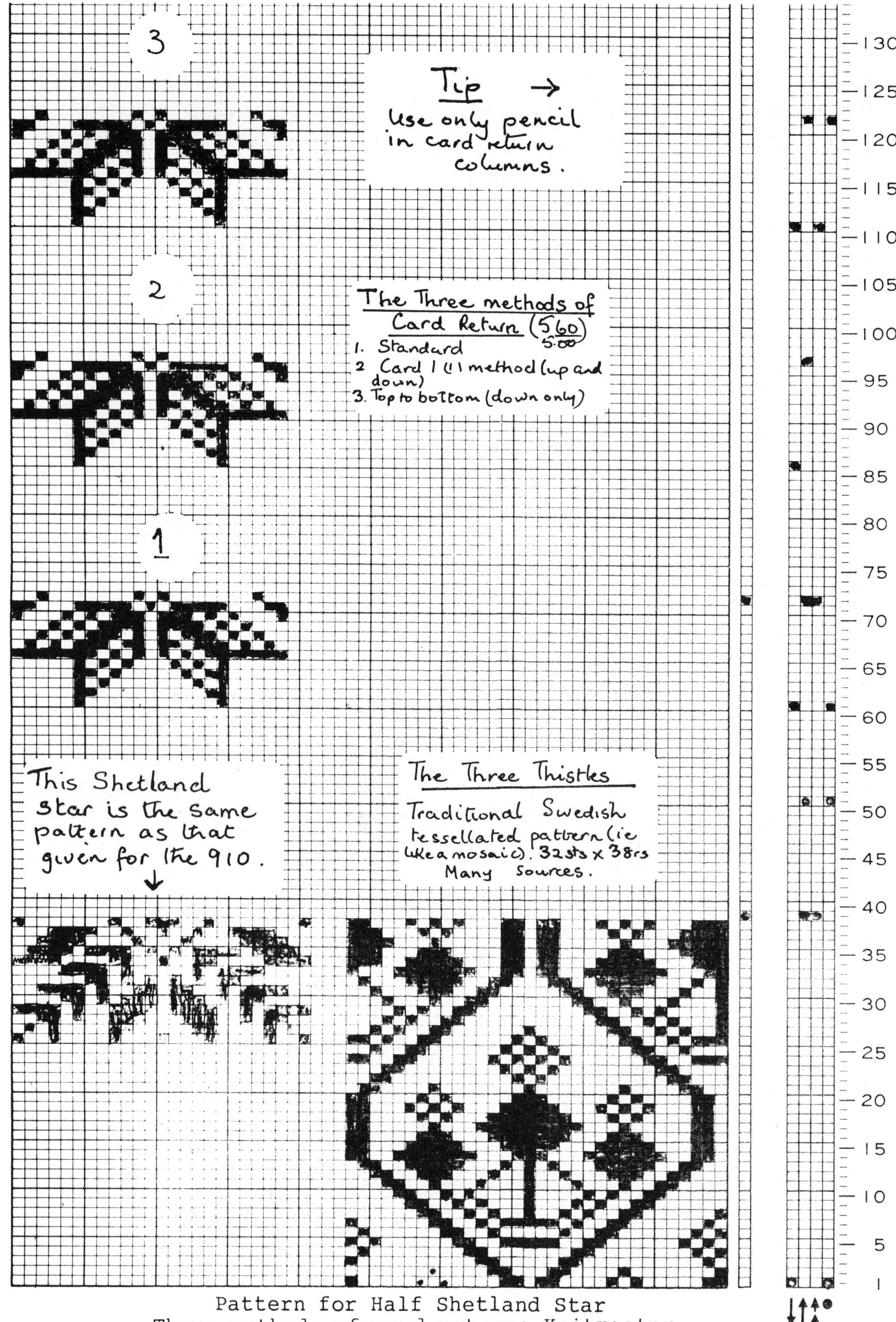
3
Tip →
Use only pencil in card return columns.
2
The Three methods of Card Return (560 / 5.00)
1. Standard
2 Card 1 (1) method (up and down)
3. Top to bottom (down only)
1
This Shetland star is the same pattern as that given for the 910.
The Three Thistles
Traditional Swedish tessellated pattern (ie like a mosaic). 32sts x 38rs
Many sources.
130
125
120
115
110
105
100
95
90
85
80
75
70
65
60
55
50
45
40
35
30
25
20
15
10
5
1

Pattern for Half Shetland Star
Three methods of card return: Knitmaster

Column 3 you mark at the bottom (to actuate quick motion to the top) and Column 4 you mark at the top (to stop quick motion). You begin this program from the top and the motif is knitted **upside down.** There is an automatic return to the top for repeat. Some laces look rather attractive when knitted upside down (see the heart pattern 2L), but choose the simple ones and use No.2 button, left hand light to correct the direction of the transfers. This method is also ideal for knitting upside down motifs on the end of a scarf, though in actual fact, when the card reaches the top of the pattern you can intervene manually by altering the direction light (press the button) as Doris Coutts described in my Second Resource Book. This is fine for one motif, but I found the pattern became muddled when I tried to repeat the procedure more than once.

Re-Marking the Existing Patterns

Cut tiny squares of self-adhesive paper (labels are suitable). Stick over the marks (in the right hand column) which you don't require. Pencil in the new marks. Use the pencils provided. Do not use silver pens. On completion, remove the sticky blobs and rub out the pencil marks with a **soft** rubber. All three methods were used in the production of the half and full star pattern, and I've used method 2 in conjunction with the mirror image to produce interesting effects in lace and weave. There are some attractive possibilities. What needs to be emphasised is that the three methods are speedy, because they require no manual intervention, once the cards have been marked.

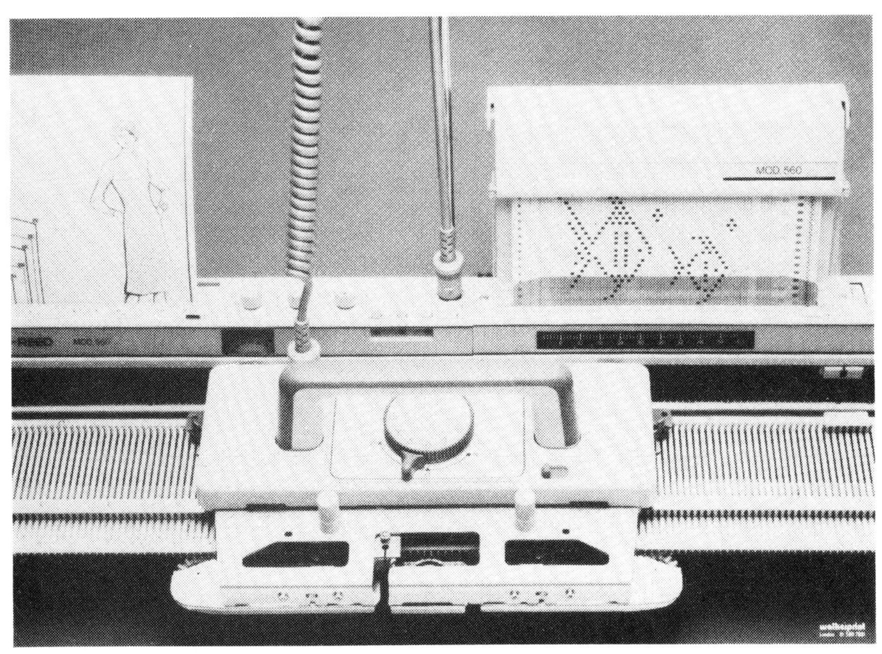

Knitmaster Lace Carriage courtesy Knitmaster

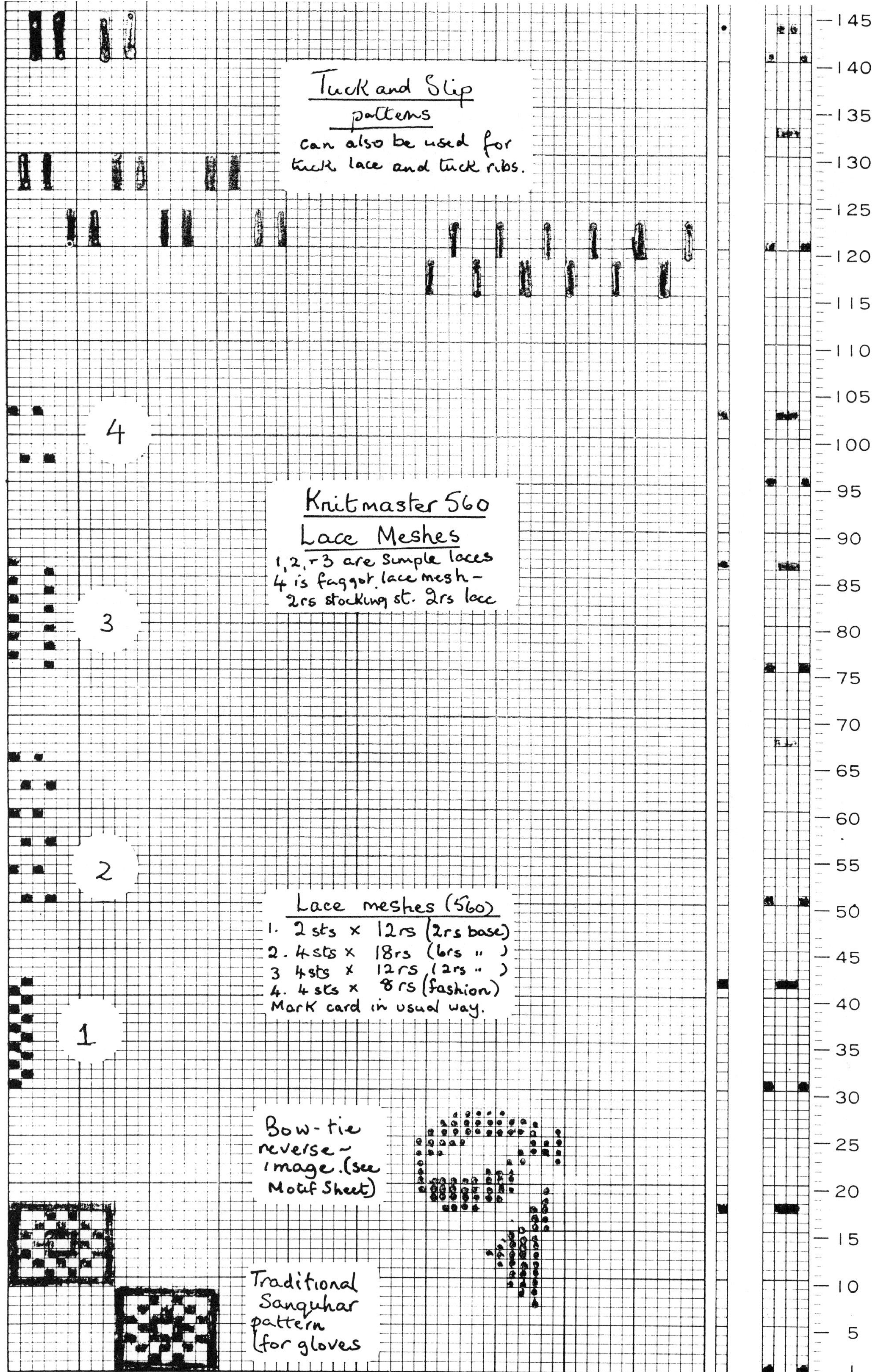

Lace Meshes 560

Lace & Cables 560

Lace and Cables (Brother 910 and Knitmaster 560)

I have included some lace meshes for you to try. The interesting point is that on an electronic machine you can have as many plain stitches between the lace patterns as you choose. This is certainly ideal for cables. The one included here was done on the Knitmaster 560 using pattern 1 of the lace meshes given on the sheet. The cables were twisted alternately (3 over 3) every 12 rows, since this made cabling easier. The result is quite pleasing.(Include 6 extra stitches in your pattern width)

Faggot Lace Mesh and the Knitmaster System

This lace mesh is the one produced most often on the Brother machines and it occurs with unfailing regularity in Nihon Vogue magazines as well as in privately published magazines and books. The latter quite often offer the same card for the same pattern and row and stitch tensions to Knitmaster knitters. Nihon Vogue on the other hand tend only to offer faggot lace mesh to Brother knitters. The identical card marked or punched for faggot lace mesh on the Brother (2 knit rows between lace rows) will produce eyelet lace, simple method, on the Knitmaster (3 knit rows between lace rows). It therefore follows that the same pattern is not produced on the Knitmaster with the identical card. To avoid frustration and disappointment, Knitmaster knitters should understand that in order to do faggot lace mesh on their machines (260-360-560) the cards must be marked or punched in the way I have shown in the Resource Book Pattern Supplement, and in this book (heart and treble disc design). The system is fashion lace,2rs knit, 2rs transfer lace. It is easy to knit and quick to do. Similar tensions and pattern appearance can then be achieved to those produced by the Brother machines. I have also included the basic faggot lace mesh (No.4) for 560 owners. Other patterns are in the Pattern Supplement. Please note, there is a tendency to drop stitches between T3 and T4 on the Knitmaster simple lace setting using a fine textured yarn and eyelet mesh. Faggot lace mesh however, providing it is carefully weighted , produces no problems.

Perhaps, some of the most attractive patterns apart from tops, featuring faggot lace mesh, are the lace skirts in Japanese magazines. On an electronic machine, you can organise the N.W.P. needles, the solid stocking stitch and the lace to suit the formation of the pleat that you have in mind without being restricted by the limits of the punchcard.

Faggot and Eyelet Lace - Historical Note

The name faggot has been borrowed from embroidery because

the cross links of yarn separating the triangular holes look very similar to faggoting. Eyelet is the older term, and was used by the 18th century framework knitters to describe any hole made by stitch transfer. The Victorians used a variety of terms or just "openwork" to describe lace stitches. Mary Thomas was the first of several authorities to sort out the muddle and give us a clear lead in differentiating faggot from eyelet lace stitches.

History isn't just interesting or fun (for some). It preserves continuity and cohesion and helps us (sometimes) to avoid chaos and confusion.

Lace Panels

You can use two sets of points cams and two sets of N.1.Cs to produce two lace panels. Do not use mirror image in this situation because a reversal of lace marks on one side means the lace carriage will transfer the stitches against the lie of the design. Choose patterns with a strong vertical interest like Card 3L(2).

No.2 Button and Mirror Image

There is an interesting example, No.61(2), (the lace butterflies) in Pattern Card set 2. The knitter is instructed to switch between left and right lights, so that the butterflies flit in one direction and then in the other, alternating their positions on the fabric. Because the design is diagonal, there is no uneven contrast in the lace structure.

There is nothing to stop us using mirror image as well as switching between lights in patterns with a diagonal lie. Switch the machine off and on again to re-program. In fact, when one considers the innumerable permutations of N.1.Cs, points cams, No.2 button (left and right lights) and mirror image, there is a wealth of interest here for the Knitmaster 560 knitter.

Offsetting a Pattern - Heart and Disc Lace Pattern (560)

Though you will find faggot lace mesh easier to knit than eyelet lace when you are using a yarn as fine as Hobby, it is good to know you have a choice.

Copy the bottom pattern on the card, and mark the right notation column for 2rs knit, 2rs fashion lace. The pattern is 60 sts wide, but it consists of two patterns each 30sts (or less) wide. You can, of course, knit only the heart pattern (26sts wide) as a repeatable pattern (T.3.2). Have the No.2 button, RH light on, and place the N.1.C. centrally over 0. Knit one repeat of the pattern. On the penultimate row, the buzzer goes. STOP. Leave the carriage outside the knitting. Move the N.1.C. 30sts exactly to the left. Count the stitches carefully. Indeed you could mark the spot beforehand. A wrong position of the N.1.C. will mean a mis-pattern in the lace mesh. Now knit the last row of the previous pattern. The card returns to the first row. During that last row, the carriage memorises the new position of the N.1.C. In the knitting rows that follow, the pattern in its offset position will appear. It is important to emphasise that the carriage memorises the new position of the N.1.C. during the course of the knitting. It is NOT necessary in this situation to put the inspection button on and memorise the N.1.C. with the carriage top in the non-knitting position. It is not difficult to remember to move the N.1.C. when the buzzer sounds, providing one moves the cam to the correct spot. The procedure is an extremely speedy one, and it is only necessary to mark the pattern out once.

Brother 910 (MKII) knitters also have a similar facility which speeds up the memorising process for offset patterns (see Note 3 under "The Three Memories" at the end of the book).

NOTE. You can program the basic faggot lace mesh from this card for a repeatable pattern. Begin on r.8. The pattern is 6sts wide and 16rs tall. Mark in pencil in the buzzer and quick motion columns.

Offsetting a Pattern. The Plume Knitweave Pattern (500-560)

The principle is the same as above. On the completion of the pattern, move the N.1.C. **half a pattern width** to the left or right. Mirror image and the Card1(1) method were used to produce the oval weave pattern. Brother 910 knitters, work out the positions for both patterns at the beginning of your knitting. You will find inputting the positions for the offset pattern quite speedy (see overall patterning from a quarter image).

Swung Stocking Stitch (910 & 560)

Because of the scope offered by the long cards and the large repeat system of the electronics, it is possible to do fashioned lace with many transfer moves, which emphasise a powerful swing of the stocking stitch pattern. Normally, the final lace holes are formed in the last one or two transfer operations. The main carriage then knits two rows over the holes. Before knitting these two rows I closed the holes by picking up from an adjacent stitch the head of the stitch below. The stitches chosen were the ones that followed the lie of the pattern. This little manual exercise on the 910 with card 10(33) took less time than cabling and was well worth the trouble. The yarn used was Patsy Amanda, a fine 3ply (T.5). Because the yarn is shiny, the swung lozenges of pattern assume a dark 3D appearance that is most attractive (developed from an idea by Susanna Lewis, New York).

NOTE. It was not possible to use the fine lace setting on this pattern. When there are multiple transfers, the fine

lace setting (on the Brother) would cause a multiple pile-up. On some patterns, it might be possible to use fine lace on the last two transfers of a sequence, but only when there is a stitch, and not just an empty needle, to receive the half stitch. In the latter situation, two needles share one stitch loop, and this produces a ladder for the rest of the knitting.
Knitmaster 560 - Try 4L(15) and 9A in the Book of Electronic Lace Patterns.

Selecting Parts of Patterns for Overall Patterning (500-560-910)

It is quite fun deciding how little of a pattern you need to use. You can also take a piece from a pattern and make a repeat from it. Knitmaster owners must choose patterns at the left hand side of the card if they want a repeatable pattern. When several lace patterns are on one sheet, put pencil marks against the relevant instruction columns to avoid confusion.

Copying a Lace Punchcard onto an Electronic Sheet

For Knitmaster owners, this is easy enough. The translation is straightforward. The exception is faggot lace mesh, as I have shown.

Brother 910 owners, begin by marking the rectangle for the two knit rows represented by the curly arrow against the LAST row of the punchcard. Then leave blank the appropriate number of rows until the next curly arrow. This is marked as a rectangle on your sheet. The holes on the punchcard are copied as marks on the mylar sheet (910 560).

NOTE. Knitmaster 560 owners, leave the yarn-change columns unmarked for simple lace. The marks for fashion lace represent stitch transfers. The blanks are knit rows.

Mylar Sheet Copies

Heat from photocopying and printing processes tends to elongate the reproduction sheets by approximately one tiny grid per 150 rows. As you trace off a pattern in this book, check that your blank mylar sheet fits the grid exactly. You may have to adjust its position every 20 rows or so.

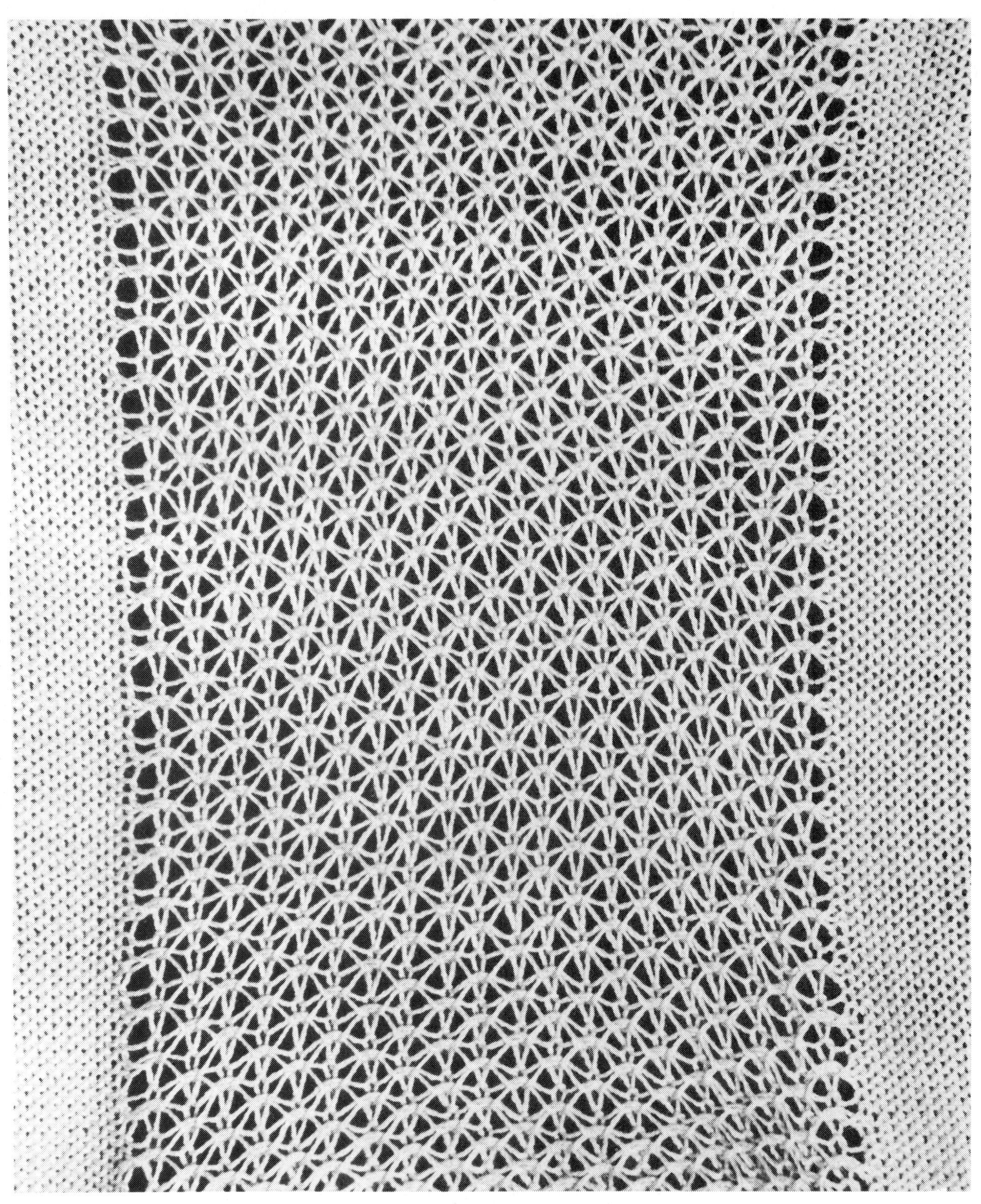

Tuck Lace Panel 910

22   A motif - Y20,Y18 (FNP), G22

38   41   Pattern Selector top,No.6 button up

19   Card 5 - 19 (Knitmaster 2(2))

1 1 0 0 1 1 ' 0 0 1 1 0 0

o

Upside Down Lace 560

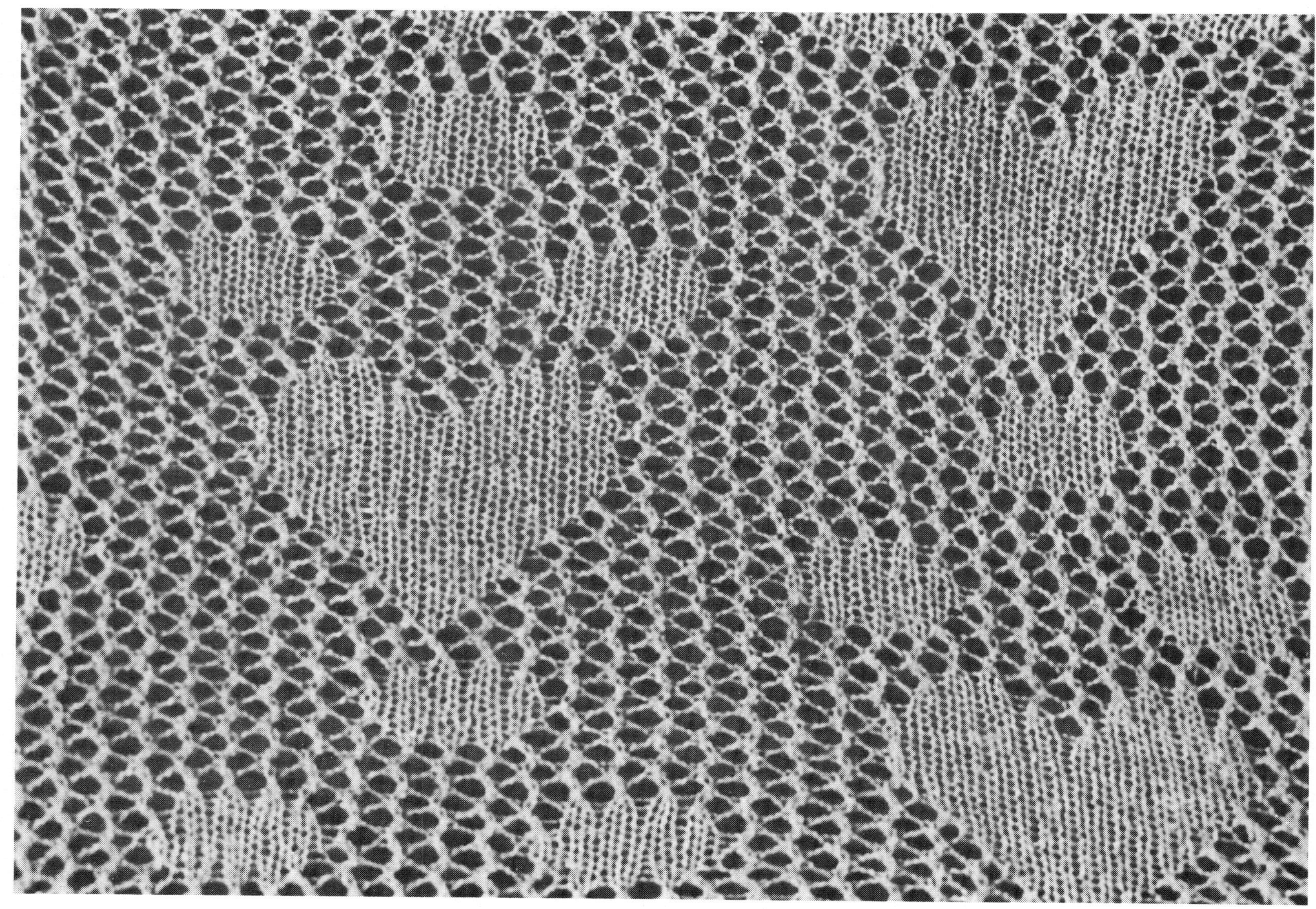

Heart & Discs Faggot Lace 560

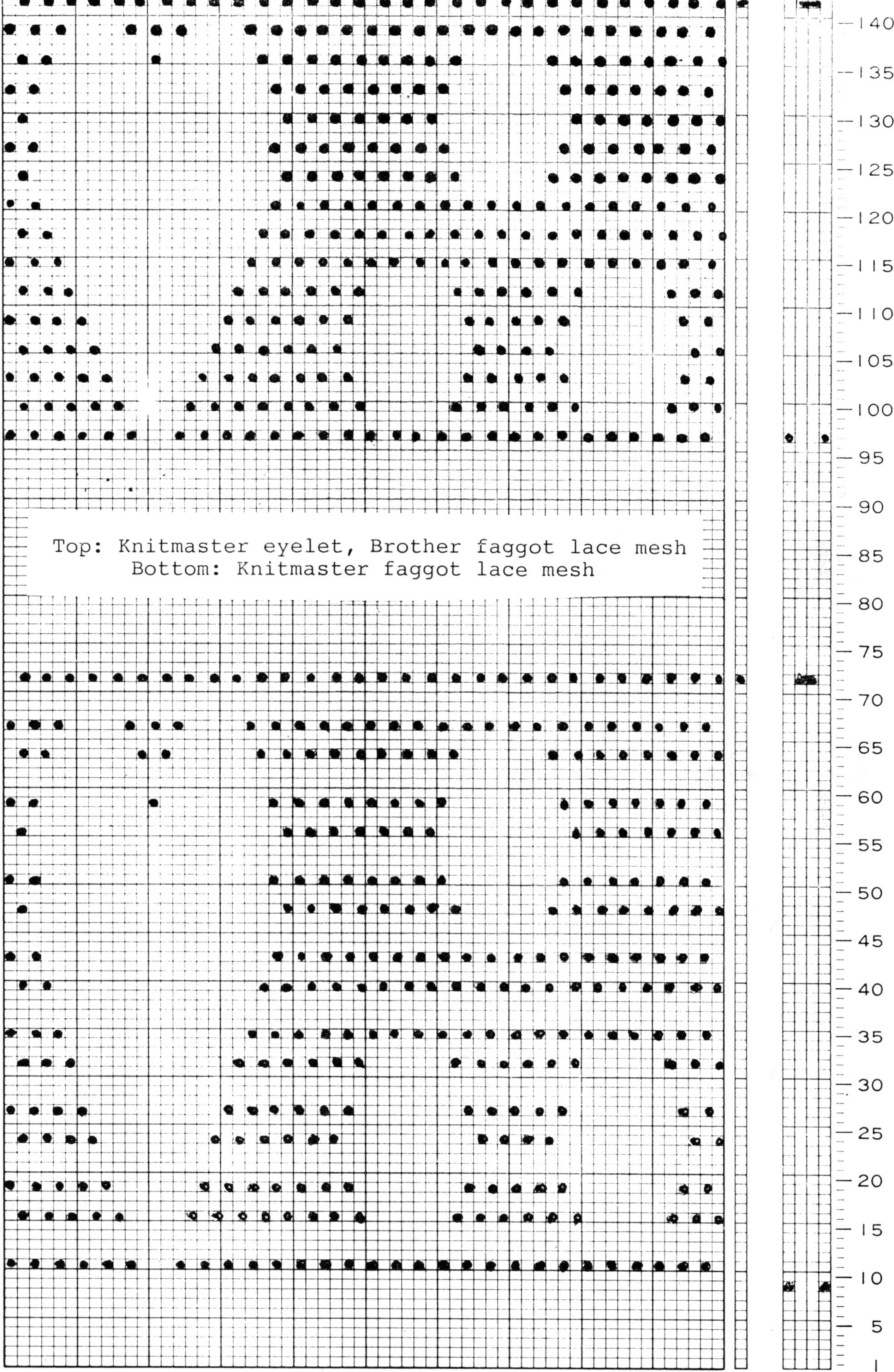

Pattern for Heart & Discs 560 910

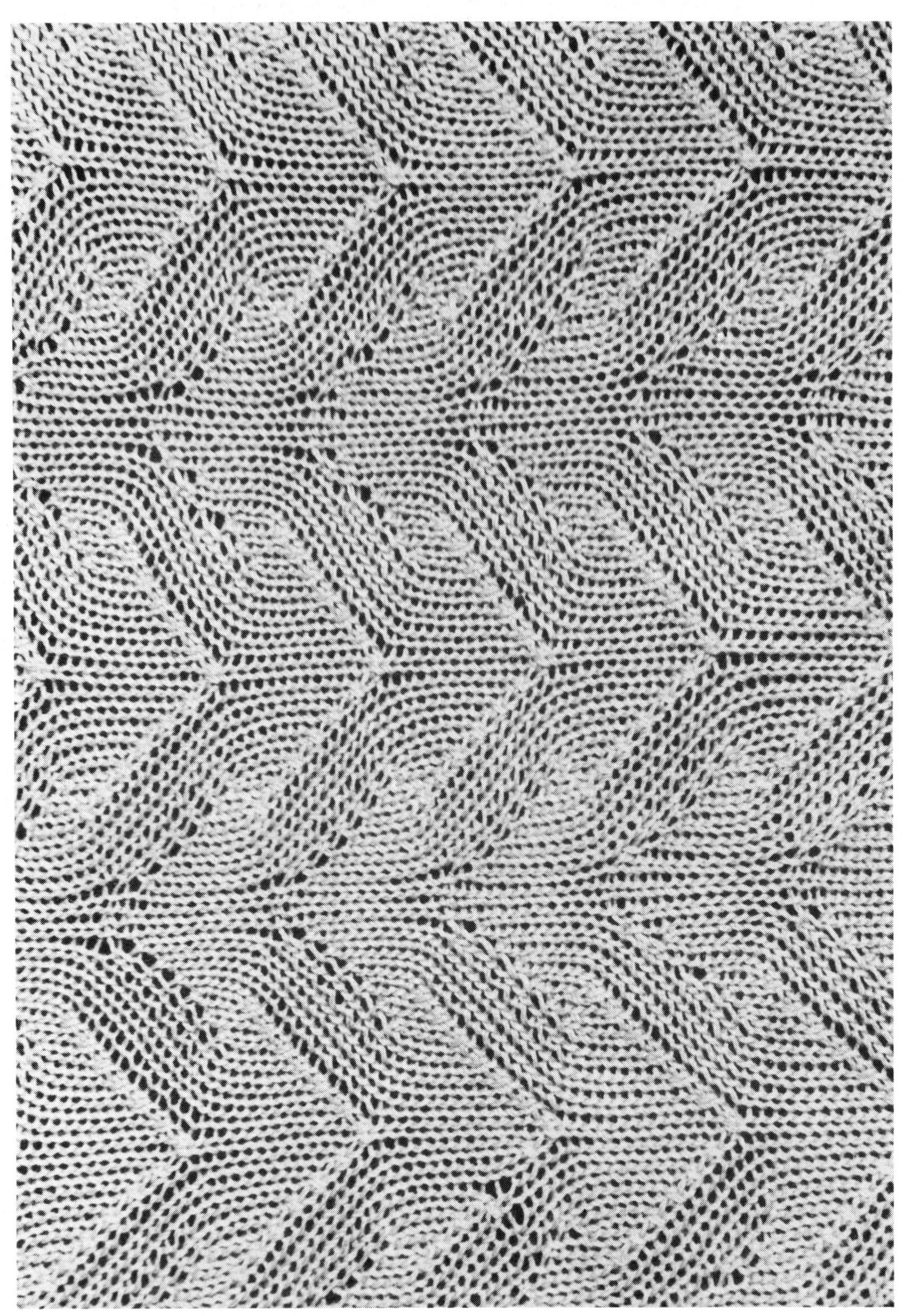

Swung Stocking Stitch 910 Card 10 (33)

Swedish Tessellated Pattern

OVERALL PATTERNING ON THE BROTHER 910

In many ways,it is rather foolhardy to attempt to deal with two electronic machines in one publication, but if they are kept separate there is real danger of isolation for one or the other. The Knitmaster and Brother machines are very different, but they have a great deal in common with regard to what they can achieve. My advice is to get with your own system and enjoy it, for there is more than enough on each machine to keep you employed for the rest of your life and longer.

There is plenty of common ground for us to be enriched by methods, techniques and patterns designed for the other machine, at least as far as overall patterning, single motifs and some of the Brother A and B facilities are concerned providing one understands the following:-

1) The pattern position and direction for overall Fair Isle and weaving on the Knitmaster Nos 1 & 2 buttons, left hand light on, can be achieved on the Brother if the No.1 switch is up (all the rest down). The motif as the Brother knitter sees it on the card will appear the same on the purl side, but study the Swedish tessellated pattern. It remains the same whichever way you look at it. Why?

2) When the 910 is set for overall patterning, the pattern is always centred on G.1.(ie. the first needle on the right of 0). This means you will get an odd number of pattern repeats. If the repeat has an odd number of stitches then G.1. is the pivot stitch, and the green half will have one more stitch than the yellow. To our eyes, what the Japanese call yellow is orange, but Y is more distinctive than O, and I have used the former in all programs.

A central pattern means an odd number of motifs across the garment. How do we get an even number? The answer is that we employ the single motif setting (pattern selector up), and program the pattern right across the bed. We can adjust at the edges just as the Knitmaster knitter adjusts with the help of the points cams. Indeed, we can organise the pattern and its separating stitches so that they match as near as possible at the seams. Our system dictates that all information is programmed into the machine. For an even number of repeats, we choose as our first needle position (FNP) Y1 or G1 at the centre.

3) The methods by which lace, tuck and slip are indicated on the cards are similar to the Knitmaster system.

a)LACE - choose fashion lace patterns for translation from the Knitmaster system. Knitmaster, begin with two knit rows, Brother, end with them. It is easy to forget these blank rows on the Brother card, and they must be programmed.

b) TUCK AND SLIP - No.6 button up is the equivalent of No.1 button,RH light on (500-560). The patterning needles are reversed and tuck and slip are marked on the card. For tuck rib and tuck lace, the Brother knitter must use KCII to ensure the first and last needles of the WP groups are not selected. Read what has been written for the Knitmaster on interpreting the punchcard correctly, though it is easier for the Brother knitter, as the overall situation on the 910 is similar to that on the punchcard machine.

The Brother 910 is a machine which has already stimulated several publications. It presents us with a vast area to be explored, and the best one can do here is to set down some of the questions knitters have asked before we look at some of the interesting options offered by both machines.

Brother 910 MKII models - please turn to the back of this book and read what is written regarding the modifications. Now carry on reading here, but remember to press the RR button on the completion of every pattern, or before a new one.

Questions and answers, hints and tips

1) How do I repeat a line of a pattern?

This question comes frequently from students who are given tuck lace patterns or the tea-cosy pattern as part of their course. On the 910, on the row before the one you wish to repeat, press the CR button. Knit across; selection will be made and the card will halt in its tracks. the light will flash all the time you pattern knit the one row.

On the row before the last, press the CE button, the light will go out and the card will move on. In fact, it is a good idea to draw a repeat of the pattern you want on the card. It doesn't take long, and after all, you can use most of the available space on the Brother 910 card.

2) How do I knit a pattern upside down?

Scarf-knitters ask this question. The page in the manual is 57. The height of the tree (30) is programmed **after** the ready light comes on. Put No.5 button up. Then the CF button is pressed. The card moves to the 30 row mark and goes down into the machine. Like the Knitmaster Card 1(1) method, there is no quick return but the buzzer speaks. If you want just 30 rows, STOP. You need to be vigilant because the card will start its return.

If you begin with the selection row from right to left, the first knitting row is from left to right, and the last knitting row will be from right to left (RC 31 = 30 plus the selection row) The figure 1 will show in the L window and the pre-select row for 1 will show in the RH column (memo window).

If you use No.5 button in the up position, the card will move to the top and then down again, exactly like Knitmaster Card1(1) method.

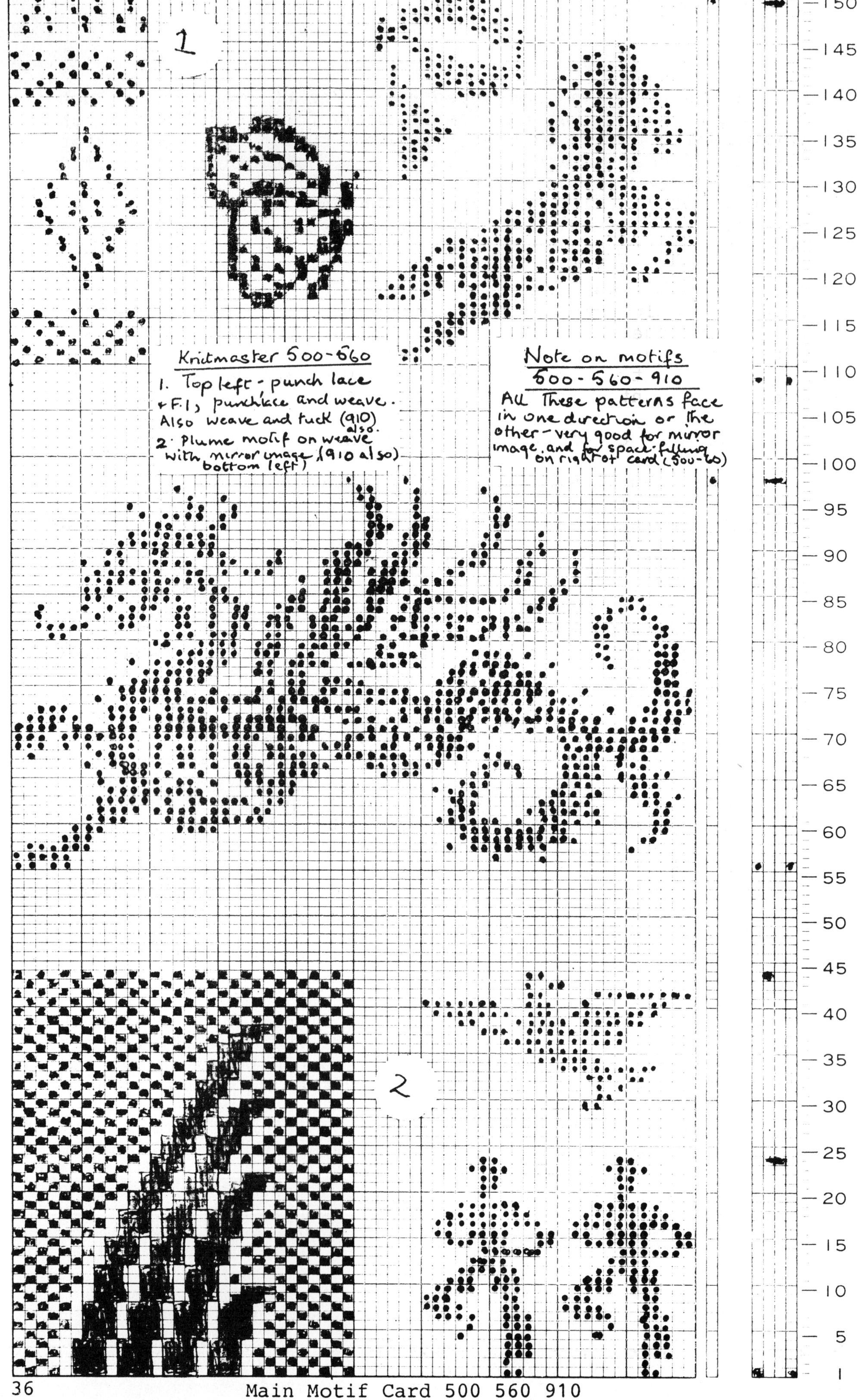

Main Motif Card 500 560 910

3) How do I insert rows of stocking stitch between patterns?

If you just want to have two to four rows of stocking stitch, it is a good idea to incorporate these on the card and program them into the machine. Change to KCII for these two rows. As soon as the needles select, it is time to begin the pattern again. On the Knitmaster you can put on the inspection button while you do stocking stitch, if you haven't included the stocking stitch rows with the pattern. On the Brother, knit your pattern. When the card has returned and the pattern is completed, switch to NL on the carriage. Knit the stocking stitch rows. The card will stay where it is until you select on KCI or II again.

4) What is the difference between the L and memo windows?

Apart from the obvious answer that the L window is used for marking knit rows between lace moves, the L window (at the left) shows the exact rows to be knitted next. The grids in the memo window are differently placed. When the L window shows 1, the memo window is one whole square below 1. The memo window is a kind of early warning system telling you that selection has to be made before the row is knitted. Sure enough, you make selection, the card stays firm, you knit the row and the card drops to 1 in the memo window, but it is on to 2 in the L window. I find it easier to mark in the L window, though we are advised to mark for exchange of colour in the memo window.

5) How do I know when a pattern has been completed?

The beeper goes. The card returns to 1 just before the knitting of the penultimate row. Knit one more row, and another. Selection is made for row 1 of the next sequence. The problems occur when we want to change the program, and a glance at the memo window will tell us exactly where we are.

6) Two cautions

a) To avoid a mis-pattern, always program with the carriage outside the left or right orange marks. Do the same when you input a new program. Take the carriage outside the marks at the end of a knitting session. The MKII model will not function at all if the carriage is wrongly placed. In actual fact, the whole carriage does not need to be outside the marks, merely the little magnet at the back should be clear of them.

b) Roll the card to the set line EXACTLY.

7) The little book, "Useful Hints for the KH 910" can be had from Brother dealers. It is an invaluable guide to what to do when you go wrong in various circumstances. I have not

attempted to deal with these in this book. Some of the newer stitch effects like lace and Fair Isle, weave and lace, and tuck and lace (do not confuse with tuck-lace), are not included in the Hints book. When pattern combinations are involved, it is best to examine the fabric and the card, and identify the row before the last one to be pulled back. Press the RR button and the card will return to the set line. Press in the correct row number noted from the L window and then the CF button. The card will advance to the correct row. Incidentally, this is an alternative method for beginning the left half of the neckline on the correct pattern row.

8) The first needle selection mechanism will not work on the lace carriage when you use the full width of the bed. You can use either 198 needles or place a 4 st. orange blocking cam at each end, which will result in 4 sts. at each end knitting plain. Orange blocking (or L) cams for the 860 - 881 can be bought separately, and can also be used in the knitting of lace inversions as an alternative to re-programming. Program an overall lace and use the L cams to block out the pattern you don't want.

9) Occasionally, a needle can get depressed under the hidden back springs of the needle bed. Quite often it will correct itself when you extend it to E. If not, set to KC and move the carriage across. If the needle doesn't move the first time, try again and it will pop out.

10) Elongation

This machine will elongate a pattern from either left or right according to where the carriage is placed. Put No.4 button up when the carriage is at the left; the card moves on at the left. Selection is made from right to left. The first knitting row is from left to right and the card goes down. The process is reversed when the carriage is at the right. When you want to change back (button 4 down), switch the machine off and on again to lose the elongation more quickly.

11) Using the single bed colour changer.

a) Elongation from the left side as above.

b) Fair Isle - Put No.6 button up to reverse the patterning needles. Study the punchcards which come with the attachment and you'll see why. The carriage is so designed to change the colours for the pattern marked in reverse to normal. Pattern knit from the left, and mark the changes in the memo window at the right.

To begin - Set to KCI,part buttons in, No 6 button up. Take carriage to right and then left. Cancel part buttons and set for F.I.

The principle is the same for multi-coloured tuck and

slip. For multi-coloured jacquard on the double bed use the part buttons (not No.7 button). Only one pattern row per colour needs to be marked when No.4 button is up.

c) Lace - Put No. 1 switch up. Operate the L carriage from the right and the main carriage from the left.

12) Finally, in overall patterning, the machine centres the pattern from a first needle position it has stored secretly in its system.

a) MKI models - if you want to discover the machine's secret, put the selector switch to the top position and press through all the data. In overall patterning we are concerned only with the little square panel representing positions on the card. Below that is an outline of a garment piece. When the pattern selector is in the top position, this representation lights up with the positions for the extent of the motif pattern on the bed, and the F.N.P. There you have it, and the machine has told its secret.

b) On MKII models, each position of the pattern selector controls a separate pattern entity, and only stores the data relating to that.

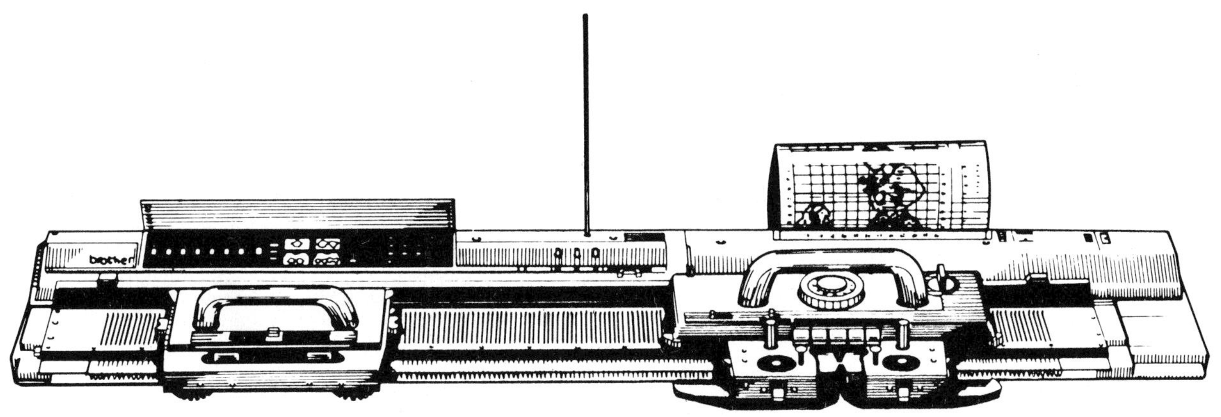

Brother 910 courtesy Brother

The Bow Tie from the Image Half 500 560

MOTIF-KNITTING ON THE KNITMASTER 500-560 AND BROTHER 910

Huge motifs in single bed F.I. can have long floats. One can, of course organise a large motif in a background of one to one F.I., but often in this situation the motif loses its impact or the pattern becomes too "busy". Various ways of dealing with long floats are given in Ch.8 of my book "Techniques in Machine Knitting" (Batsford). One good way is to cut long floats and knot them as I have done on the back of the animal swatch.

Recently I have been experimenting with crocheting up the floats and stitching the crochet chain down with invisible thread. One can also use a sewing machine to stitch invisibly on the right side in the grooves between the stitches. Though this forces the stitches apart a little, on the wrong side the floats are held in place. One also needs to deal with gaping edge stitches either by wrapping or by main colour neatening yarn. In fact, both methods need to be employed.

When one has a motif 60 sts wide there are problems if the Knitmaster knitter uses mirror image. Take the large dragon motif. We would have to de-claw him by one vertical line of stitches, or de-tail him by seven, to avoid his being glued to an adversary, depending on which light (No. 2 button) we use.(see photo of swatch) On the Knitmaster then, it is important to leave the appropriate space on the card at the beginning or end of the motif if one is going to use mirror image (Button 5). In the case of half an image, like the bow tie we would leave no space at the knot side. On the Knitmaster one gets an exact double image and no overlap to create a pivot stitch. With two sets of PCs and two N.1.Cs, there is variety as we shall see.

Motif Knitting and Mirror Image on the Knitmaster 500-560

There are three places where we can put the N.1.Cs within the limits set by the PCs.

1) In or near the middle
2) At the extreme left under the left PC
3) At the extreme right under the right PC

We need to consider direction, and whether we need to use the left or right light (button 2), though I have had a mis-pattern when I have moved from right to left light and haven't double-checked the new program by passing the carriage four times over the bed. This situation occurred when I was using two sets of PCs and two sets of N.1.Cs (the second set of PCs slide on from the left side under the Knitradar). I now find it is safer to switch off and on again and then re-program. This can be done very speedily if there are stocking stitch rows separating the motifs.

Switch off and on again to the new light position before the stocking stitch rows so that the machine can memorise the position before the pattern starts again.

Mirror Image (Button 5)

The N.1.C. is the focal point. Whether one uses the left or the right light of button 2, it is the left image that is turned round. Mirror image on the Knitmaster (single pair or repeatable) is very easy to do, and offers quite a variety of options.

When the left light is on - the image is back to back or end to end under the central N.1.C.

When the right light is on - the image is front to front or one to one, under the central N.1.C.

Two catch phrases:-

Left is left for end to end.
Right is right for one to one.

Look at the experiments with the bow tie (image half)

Copy the image half onto the card twice.

1) With the half knot against the extreme left edge of the card (as per motif card).

2) With the reverse image of the half knot turned towards the right (see lace mesh card)

These are the two positions for an image half, or indeed for any motif facing left or right. Now begin to experiment with different positions of the N.1.C., PCs and left and right lights of button 2.

Hint - You can change colours mid-row if your motifs are more than 24 sts apart, but on the Knitmaster you must be quick and not keep the carriage still for more than 30 secs or else it will mis-pattern. You can change colours for the little dancing men. One foot (embroider the other), trousers, head and hat can all be different colours.

Image half. Position 1.

You will get a perfect image when:-

1) The left light is on and the N.1.C. is under the right PC.

2) The right light is on and the N.1.C. is under the left PC.

3) The right light is on and the N.1.C. is in the centre.

Image half. Position 2.

You will get a perfect image when:-

1) The left light is on and the N.1.C. is in the centre.

2) The right light is on and the N.1.C. is under the left PC.

3) The right light is on and the N.1.C. is under the right PC.

Fair Isle is not the only pattern where we can use mirror image. In the weaving and lace examples which follow in the last section, I used Card 1(1) method in conjunction with mirror image to get an overall pattern. The new weaving arm is a delight to use on the 560, and it is a pity we cannot fix it on the 500. Remember too that you can shift the pattern along the bed, so there are quite a few options to try.

With two sets of PCs and a judicious placing of two N.1.Cs you can have two large dragons (60 sts wide), face to face with the space of one PC between! Place the N.1.Cs under left and right PCs respectively, left hand light and button 5 mirror image. In fact you could have three dragons if you had stitches, one facing two. No de-clawing would be necessary.

It is worth playing around with two images in contrasting poses on the sheet, using the two sets of PCs and N.1.Cs, with or without mirror image, and this is what I have done with the two little dancing men. In fact you have a situation here similar to that provided by one of the facilities of the A & B motif setting on the Brother 910.

Using the right hand side of the card (Knitmaster)

One can only use patterns at the extreme left hand side of the card and any combinations from there towards the right, to create a repeatable pattern, but one can use empty spaces at the right for single motifs and panels. The sample with the two little dancing men was knitted from the original card in this book. It is of vital importance to plan the positions of your motif groups. Use your fingers to arrange the needles and note the spaces between motifs and the positions of the PCs and the N.1.Cs before you begin to knit.

There are two ways one can knit a motif on the right of the Knitmaster card. In both, the pattern width indicator is set at 60.

1) Set the PCs to enclose the width of the motif. Look at the sheet and count. Do not be put off by the width indicator. Put the N.1.C. under the left PC, No. 2 button, LH light on. This method has limitations and is not as versatile as the next one.

2) Set up as above, but this time have the mirror image button 5 on, and put the N.1.C. under the PC of your choice.

I used two sets of PCs and two N.1.Cs for the little men and found I achieved considerable variety as you can see, partly because the motif consisted of two identical figures. Even more variety could be achieved if the figures were placed in contrasting poses. To return to the little men: in the first series, the N.1.Cs were placed under the right and left PCs respectively (moving from left to right on the bed). In the second series, one man only, the N.1.Cs were reversed. Next time, I switched on the No.2 button RH light, and got to my astonishment the weaving pattern at the extreme left of the card. Then I realised that the RH light was bound to fix on the first stitch of the pattern width. I switched back immediately and the little men became matadors waiting behind a barrier for the bull to come their way!

Electronic machines, as we can see, are full of surprises, most of them quite delightful. This mistake could prove to be a great discovery when I have had time to explore it.

A little discovery - when you are using two sets of PCs and N.1.Cs, mirror image, and want to alternate between lights on button 2, put on the inspection button. The card comes up. Press button 2. Push off the inspection button. The row and light change are memorised. I had no trouble here though I did not take this precaution. On other occasions I wish I had.

Two Knitmaster Specialities.

1) Weaving and Punchlace (see top left of motif sheet)

This is something we never do and yet if we choose the colours with care we can achieve interesting and delicate effects. With the same pattern it is possible to do Fair Isle or tuck with punchlace as well as weaving and tuck (Brother 910 also).

2) Two needle tucks.

Because of the method of stitch production, the Knitmaster machines tackle two needle tucks efficiently. You can have considerable variety as you have the whole 60 st. repeat to explore. What is more, the pattern could be planned as a single stitch tuck and you could then use No. 4 button for horizontal expansion to get the two needle effect. Two needle tucks give a bold geometric pattern with an interesting texture to contrast with the colour effects.

A final point - when one is using two sets of PCs and two N.1.Cs one can space them apart in any chosen width. The pattern within the limits of the PCs will be correct. The Knitmaster then has considerable free style possibilities in this situation.

Little Dancing Men 500 560

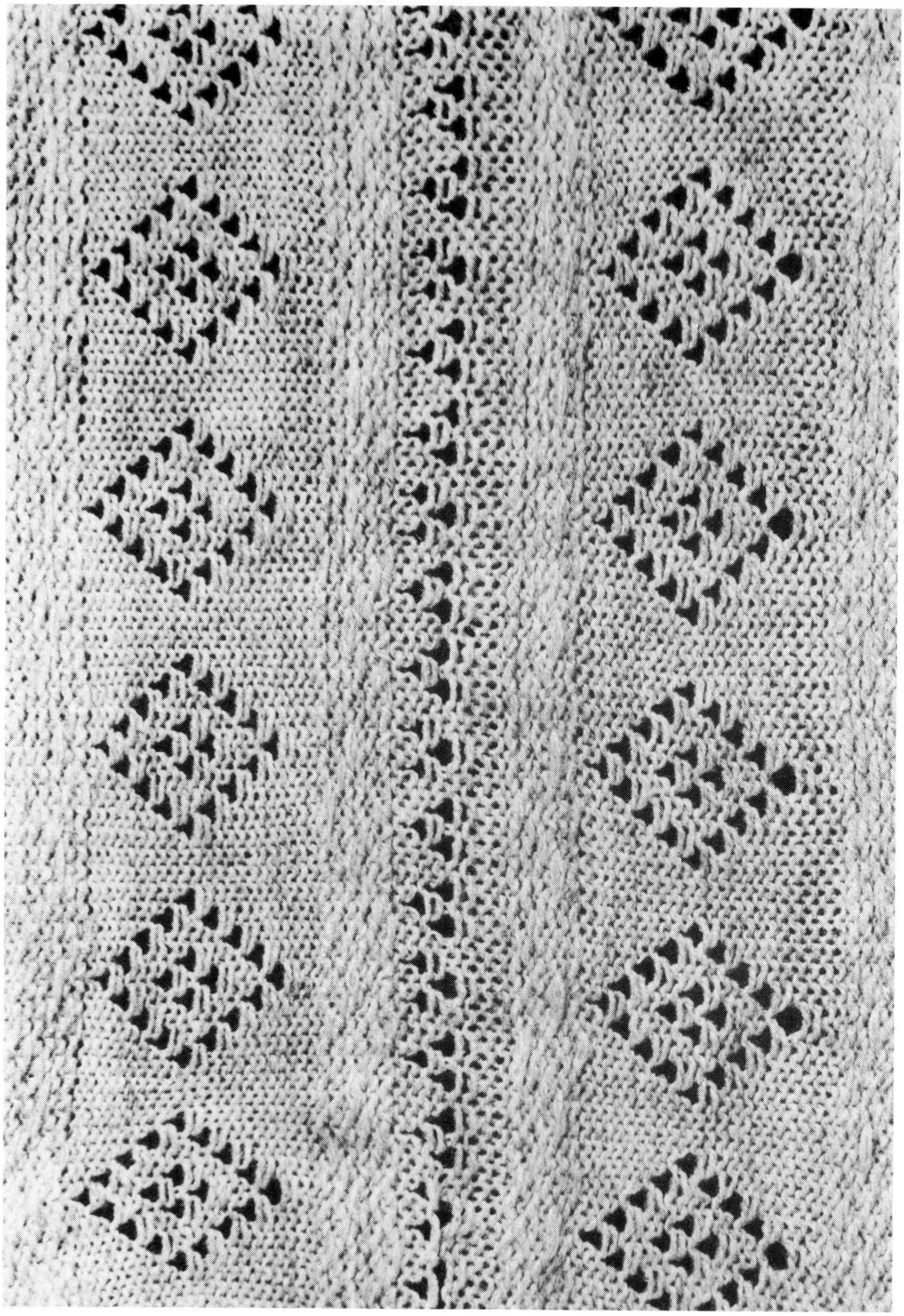

Weaving & Punch Lace 500 560

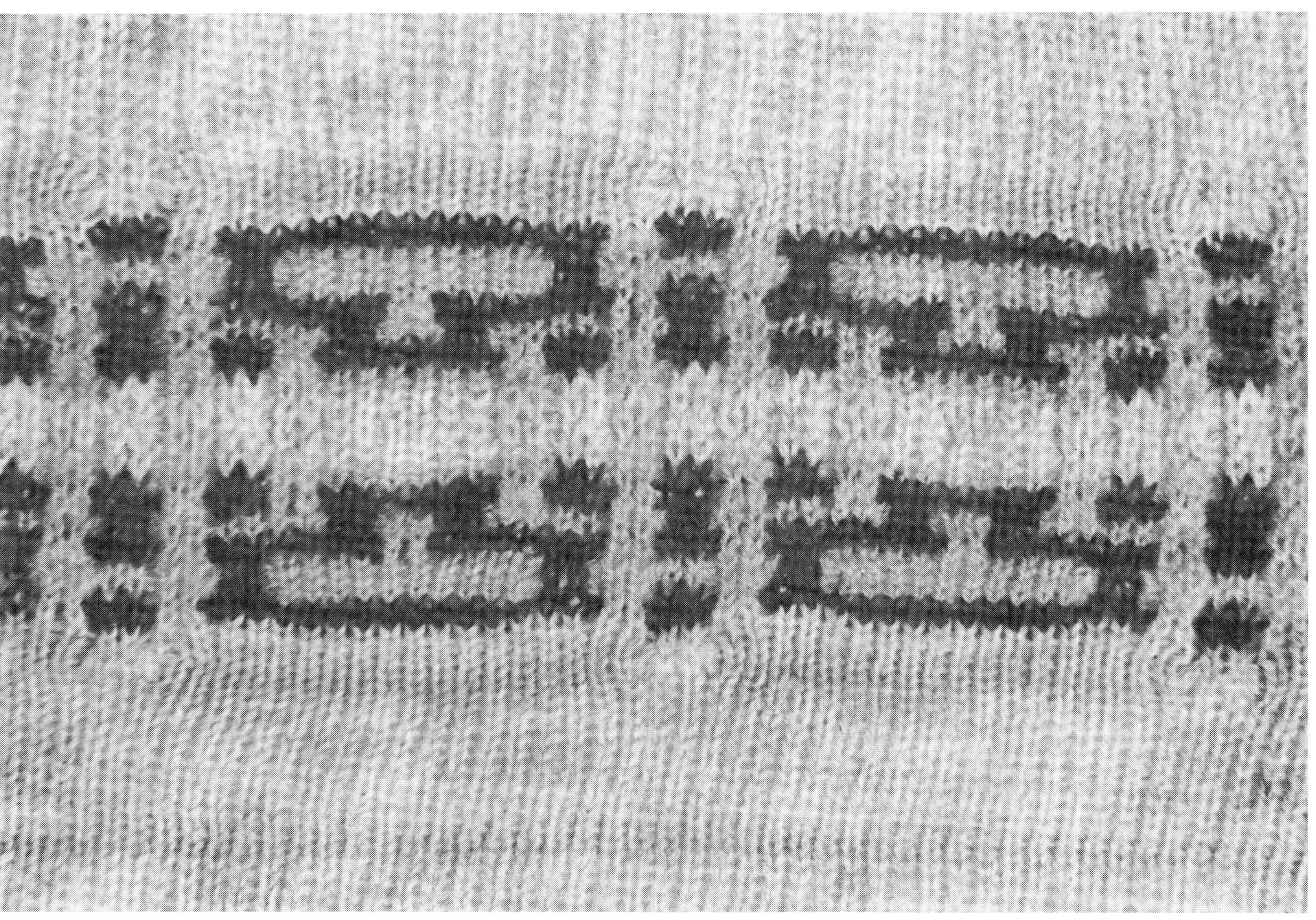

Two Needle Tuck 500 560

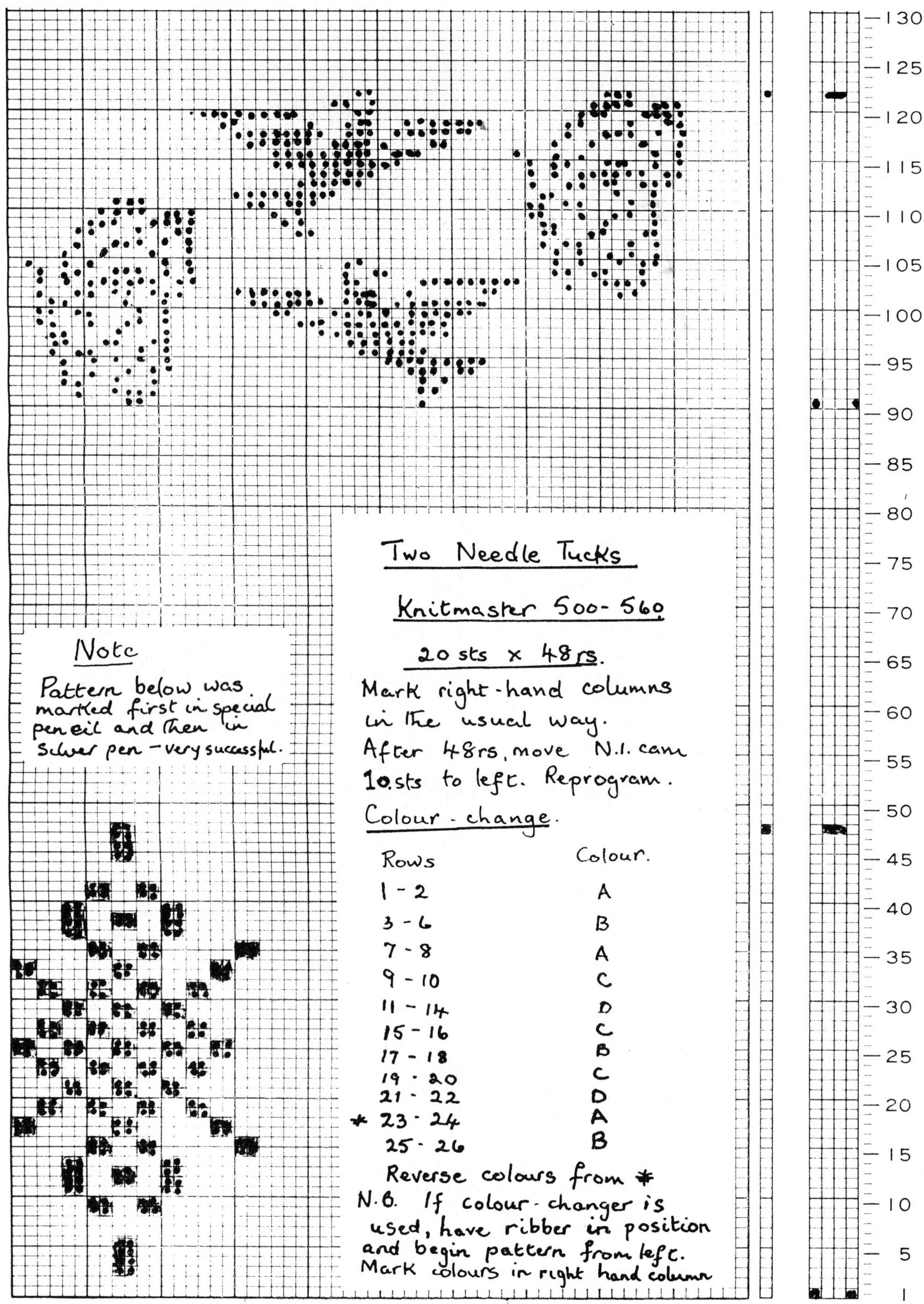
Two Needle Tucks
Knitmaster 500-560
20 sts x 48rs.
Mark right-hand columns in the usual way.
After 48rs, move N.1. cam 10.sts to left. Reprogram.
Colour - change.
Rows Colour.
1 - 2 A
3 - 6 B
7 - 8 A
9 - 10 C
11 - 14 D
15 - 16 C
17 - 18 B
19 - 20 C
21 - 22 D
* 23 - 24 A
25 - 26 B
Reverse colours from *
N.B. If colour-changer is used, have ribber in position and begin pattern from left.
Mark colours in right hand column
Note
Pattern below was marked first in special pencil and then in silver pen - very successful.
130
125
120
115
110
105
100
95
90
85
80
75
70
65
60
55
50
45
40
35
30
25
20
15
10
5
1

Pattern for Two Needle Tuck

BROTHER 910 - A AND A & B MOTIFS.

This machine is probably more like a computer than any other machine on the market. One suspects that even its Japanese inventors have realised only a fraction of its capabilities. Several of the options here are not in any manuals. Knitters are discovering all kinds of possibilities as they knit.

While most new knitters find overall patterning and A (single) motifs easy to accomplish, the A & B setting remains for many a closed book, yet it is this setting which is the most exciting of all.

A motif - (Pattern switch - up position)

We can take a motif or a combination of motifs from anywhere on the sheet and use one or both, singly or in multiples across the bed. KCII is employed as we do not want the end needles to select. As we have pointed out already we choose the FNP on the bed. There are four points we must bear in mind, which are important in the programming of A or single motifs.

1) The FNP is determined by the end mark of the motif NEAREST TO THE LEFT SIDE OF THE CARD. If you wish the motif to appear **on the purlside** as it is on the card, then you program as for the fish on p.46 of the manual 1 - 19, so you could choose Y19 as your FNP on the bed, finishing at Y1. Y19 is the equivalent of 1 on the pattern sheet. Both are left positions. Supposing however, you wish to have the fish turned round, (No,1 button up,). The FNP on the card is still its snout, but on the bed the tail end will be the FNP. Should you not program the position on the card as 19 - 1, instead of 1 - 19, since the tail is going to be at the left? Try it and see. You will find the fish has knitted perfectly, tail towards the left, and it looks as if the machine has submitted to your will. Press through the program again, and you will see that the machine has quietly turned around your correction. It flashes 1 - 19 at you. There is an important lesson here.

On single motif (pattern selector up), the first position at the left in the program is as on the card, whether the No.1 button is up or not.

Think of it in two stages - one, as the motif is on the card, and two (only after you've programmed), that you want the motif turned round. Now put up No.1 switch.

TO SUM UP - The FNP and the first needle at the left of the motif on the bed are usually one and the same (with an A motif). It is still so when the motif is in the green part of the bed. Go through your pattern manuals and check (see the two squirrels p.10 Pattern manual).

2) How do I knit one and a bit motifs?

This is a strange question, but it refers to the lace pattern Card 10 -34 of which only two-thirds seem to be on the card. Joy Greig, writing in the New South Wales seminar notes (1982) was the first to deal with it. I have also had similar queries.

This lace design is fine for a repeatable pattern, but if one wishes to knit a panel of a diamond flanked by two trellis patterns, then one needs another trellis pattern to complete. Turn to p.63 of the instruction book and p.10 of the pattern manual, and study the tree flanked by a squirrel on either side. The motif is one tree and one squirrel (1 - 60 on the card), but the extent is over 90 sts. Here is one of the exceptions to the rule that the FNP and first working needle at the left are one and the same. The half motif is 30 sts to the left of the FNP.

Go back to your lace pattern 10 - 34 and study the arrangement of 1 - 22 sts, but you need 3 extra sts at the left. Two panels of this pattern look very attractive. (see photo) You plot the pattern as A & B motifs (see basic representations of A & B motifs) Pattern Selector (middle)

Program for Lace Panels Card 10 - 34

```
     150            A motif - Y34,Y31 (FNP),Y10
 1         22                 B motif - 1 -22
      91            B motif - G10,G13 (FNP),G34
```

Note - There are 18 sts between the panels. Choose your own width according to where you want the panels to be. Plan their position on the Knitleader sheet.

3) When you knit multiples of single motifs you must also include in the width, the space between each one. If you have used horizontal expansion (No.3 button up), then double the width must be programmed plus double the space between each motif on the card.

4) Overall Patterning using the Pattern Switch in the Up Position.

Here we have the second exception to the rule regarding the FNP. Usually, when we use the single motif position for overall patterning we program the FNP as G1 or Y1. Why? Because we go to this method when we want an equal number of pattern repeats on either side of 0, and also it is one which can remain constant no matter how much shaping we may do at the sides.

Many lace knitters, as well as those who do F.I., use the single motif method because they can program all but the last two needles on either side. The lace carriage only passes the first and last needles. Having two edge needles knitting all the time means a neater seam. The only problem is that when we come to shaping, we have to re-program. How do we do it?

To re-program from the same pattern (lace)

The beeper goes and the card returns to half a tiny grid below the 1 mark in the L window. STOP. Input the new program. Knit across. The last row of the old program is knitted, and the first row of the new one is selected (see also program for filet lace under Superimposition, for an explanation p.82).

To re-program from the same pattern (not lace)

Knit ONE MORE ROW after the card returns.i.e. the row before selection for row 1 is made. Now input the new program and begin. If you are starting from a different row than row 1, press in the number and CF.

Additional notes

1) Both the above programs work on the 910 MKII without pressing the RR button. For a new pattern on a different part of the card, you will need to press the RR button (MKI & II).

2) Remember to move the carriage outside the orange marks BEFORE you press the RR button. This is an essential operation for every new program or re-program.

3) The single motif setting for allover patterning is of course suitable for tuck or slip, as you can see by the pattern on p.28. It is important that the No.6 button is up or else there will be a muddle. An exception to the rule is the marking for skirt shaping (see p.91).

4) The data in the memory store will not produce the right design unless the correct card and pattern are set to knit. An old pattern is wiped out immediately a new one is superimposed. Data stored on one setting of the pattern selector cannot be used by the patterning system if one of the other two settings is in use (MKII).

The 910 Pattern Selector.

Key to card and needle bed representations

1) Bottom position - A motif, overall patterning centred on G1.The plottings are illuminated on the card representation at the TOP LEFT ONLY.

2) Top position - A motif, choice of FNP. The plottings

are illuminated on the card representation at the TOP LEFT, and on the garment - needle bed representation at the BOTTOM LEFT.

3) Middle position - A & B motifs, choice of FNPs.
A motif - as No.2 above.
B motif - the plottings are illuminated on the card representation (horizontal limits only) at the TOP RIGHT, and on the garment needle bed representation at the BOTTOM RIGHT.

Additional notes

a) In 2 & 3 above, you choose and press the colour button Y or G BEFORE you can program the FNP and pattern limits.

b) On the pattern panel, the house and the tree symbols face different directions when the buttons are up as opposed to down.

Reversing the image

No.1 button up (A motif, House symbol) The image as you see it on the card will be reversed on the purl side of the fabric. Use the up position for letters and numbers. The A button is operative when the pattern selector is in the top or bottom positions and is operative for the A motif only when the pattern selector is in the middle position.

No.2 button up (B motif, Tree symbol) The B button is operative only for the B motif when the pattern selector is in the middle position.

Mirror image - single pair and repeats. Choose one of the above options. To knit the animal groups on the large swatch, have No.1 button up. For the little horse, leave the right half of the card empty in order to plot the mirror image repeat (see A & B motifs).

Key to Pattern Buttons (Right Side)

M Memory button

When you press this button, each of the tiny red spots on the card and /or garment representations lights up in turn. At the second press, the purple number display panel stays blank, Input the number, press the M button and the illuminated red spot moves on. If you do not input a number and press the M button again, a number previously memorised will show up and will indeed act on the pattern card. Check through the numbers at the end of an input session by pressing the M button all through the program.

CE Cancel entry

Any wrong entry can be cancelled immediately by pressing this button. The purple display panel is empty. Input the

Brother 910 Pattern Panel

new number and press M. The CE button also cancels the red error light when it flashes.

CR Cancel Row.

This is the opposite to CF. Press in a number, say 2, on the panel. Press CR, two rows are subtracted and the card moves back two rows. If you press the CR button and do not press in a number, the error light flashes and the card halts. This is the equivalent of locking the punchcard and repeating a pattern row.

RR Row Return.

The RR button takes the card back to the set line and to a neutral position. This is one reason why it is important to press it on the MKII models after every pattern is completed. Press the RR button and the card returns to the set line. Switch off the machine and remove the card.

MKII. If you switch off the machine and remove the card without using the RR button, you will find that when you put in a new card the error light flashes and the card refuses to move when you press CF. Press CE, then RR. Switch off and on again. The card will now move forward when CF is pushed.

CF Card Forward

If the CF button is pushed, the card goes automatically to row 1. If you press in a number, say 16, and then CF, the card goes to row 16 and stops.

PLEASE NOTE - Numbers pressed in on CR and CF are instructions to the card only. As the M button is not pressed these numbers are not retained by the memory store.

REMEMBER

Only the data that relates to the setting of the pattern selector in use will be acted upon.

Press through your program and check it is correct. If you have inserted a different pattern card, and the input data refers to another, you will get a pattern alright, but it will be decidedly scrambled and wrong. If the data fixes on the blank part of the wrong card, you will get no pattern at all. If you remove the (correct) card before the pattern knitting is complete, make a note of which card it is and at which row in the L window you begin. At the next knitting session, roll the card to the set line. Press in the row number and CF.

Some Queries Answered.

1) The memory for the card readings and for the next row of pattern is held until the batteries expire and 888 flashes in the panel (MKI), or for at least 3 weeks (MKII). If you return to the MKII model after a long absence, press through the pattern with your finger on the M button. If a series of 1s appears the pattern has gone. You will have to re-enter the data. Always check the pattern after a break.

2) There is no need to remove the card if you haven't finished the pattern at the end of a knitting session, providing you are returning within a few hours. Switch off the machine, leaving the card where it is. When you return, check that the carriage is outside the orange marks. Switch on the machine and carry on knitting (MKI & II). The principle is the same when you want to knit a wedge of stocking stitch between patterns and haven't included it on the card.

3) The green power switch light in the middle at the back appears and stays on when you switch on the current. It is not necessary for the carriage to pass the green light on every pattern row, but it is necessary for the magnet on the

back of the carriage (main or lace) to pass over the grey rectangular piece of metal set on the runner track below the central position of the row counter (ie at G1).

If you are working at the extreme right or left of the bed, say on a triangular shawl, the card will not move on unless the carriage is taken to a point where the magnet can pass the centre (see p.43 of the instruction manual).

4) You can cancel the no first needle selection mechanism underneath the lace carriage (as on the 860 - 881) by turning the screws in the orange cams, left for left and right for right, to ensure that the first needles can select.

It is only necessary to make this mechanical alteration when both main and lace carriages are patterning during the knitting of a lacy skirt, where NWP needles form the inner pleat, and a slip or tuck stitch forms the outer one. First needle selection means that the edge stitches before and after a NWP needle gap will knit and not slip or tuck outside the pattern. Turn the screws back to their original position on completion.

A AND B MOTIFS

Imagine a draughtsman's empty board hidden away inside the machine. On it there is a tiny graph-grid space for every needle, double the height and the width of the pattern capabilities i.e. 300 x 400. As you program your pattern from the 60 st. repeat system, it is plotted by an invisible hand on the board. If you have programmed an unworkable setup knittingwise, the machine will oblige and churn it out as a muddled up pattern. The responsibility is yours. "Operator fault", as the Japanese say. Where do you begin? There is one definition and there are two rules.

THE DEFINITION:

The Brother 910 is the only current machine which will allow the knitter to program and knit simultaneously on one horizontal level two patterns or pattern groups, subject to two separate sets of instructions. As a simple example, you can knit the main part of a jacket in one pattern and the front border in another in one operation.

THE TWO RULES

1) The A motif can be left or right on the card, but it must always be the TALLER of the two. This is why only the grid readings for the horizontal limits of the B pattern are required. In most cases, the A motif emerges as the dominant pattern. The A & B patterns can be the same height

Brother 910 Lace Panels(10 - 34)

and the A motif can also serve as the B motif.

2) For every mirrored pattern, whole, half or in part that is programmed to repeat across the bed, there must be the appropriate space on the sheet and space on the needlebed of the machine. This must not be forgotten especially when:

a) the A serves as the B motif as well, and

b) the B motif is the invisible partner in a mirror image repeat pattern.

In this book we shall look at briefly:

a) Basic representations of A & B motifs.
b) Mirror image: A is for B.
c) Picture style arrangements.
d) Diagonals: overlap, mirror and reflection images.
e) Overall patterning from a quarter image.
f) Superimposition.
g) Automatic shaping using slip (part).

NOTE: The pattern selector is in the MIDDLE position.

a) Basic representations of A & B motifs.

Take No.3 card out of your pack and look at 3 - 12, the house and the tree. These are the easiest to start with as: - 1) they are the symbols of the A and B motifs in the overall patterning position on the card panel (buttons down). 2) The pattern is 60sts wide, 30rs high, each motif being 30sts wide. Nothing could be easier.

Most of the swatches I have knitted for the photos are 100sts wide. Choose a position for your A motif (house), and one for your B motif (tree). Here is my program.

```
      30          A motif - Y35,Y35 (FNP),Y5
  1        30                B motif - 31 - 60
       1          B motif - G5,G5 (FNP), G35
```

The fact that I chose to have 10sts between motifs is a small indication of the freedom one has in programming A & B motifs. Next I chose to overlap the images by 6sts (see the instruction manual pp.49 & 69). The program for pattern A was Y15,Y15 (FNP), G15. For pattern B, G10,G10 (FNP),G40. Notice how pattern A is the dominant one in the overlap. I've gone round the edge of the tree with Swiss darning to give a slightly stand-off effect. Finally, I put the pattern switches up (1 & 2) and reversed the programs to G15,G15 (FNP), Y15 for motif A, and Y10,Y10 (FNP), Y40 for motif B. Try these exercises and you will begin to understand a little of the freedom you have.

b) Mirror image: A is for B.

This is the horizontal version of reflection. Because we can decide the distance between the pattern and its image, we are dealing with TWO SEPARATE DESIGN ENTITIES, though in fact one pattern on the card serves as both A and B motifs.

1) Single motif.

This is the easiest to tackle. Study the example on p.55 of the manual, right hand side. Notice that the first motif (A) is in the green section, and the B motif (the fish in reverse) is in the yellow section. You can do the same arrangement more logically by reversing the A motif (No.1 button up). Try Y20,Y20 (FNP), Y2, and the B motif, G2,G20 (FNP), G20. (2sts between fish snouts)

When the FNP is at the right of the motif (G20) instead of the left, the chances are that you will get a mispattern at the widest part. Now, try G2 instead of G20 and you should have a perfect reproduction. For knitters who can't work problems out on paper, sitting at the machine and pushing out needle arrangements is the best way. Remember that a space at the side of a motif will be doubled in a mirror image.

NB. You can make a single motif mirror image from any pattern on the card JUST ONCE i.e. a single pair, without having to plot an empty space on the card.

2) Mirror image: single motif repeats.

Study the little fishes under the swan and cygnets (see photo). There is no example in the manuals that come with the machine, but there is one on p.19, B1 of Variation Patterns in the Supplementary pack. What is so easy on the Knitmaster is a little more difficult here. It is not possible on the 910 to do a series of mirror image repeats with motifs wider than 29sts on the card. It is unlikely that you would wish to do so. Turn to the fishes again, Card 4 - 17.

You cannot use the large fish as it is on the card, but you can use the small fish for this exercise. Why?

At the right side of the small fish is a space large enough for his mirror image to be plotted on the machine's invisible drawing board. The filled and the empty spaces together make up the complete width of the program. I use pages from an A4 knitter's graph pad to help me plot this kind of pattern, but usually manipulating the needles at the machine does the trick. If you don't attempt any other exercise in this book, please try this one if you wish to understand and use the potential of the 910's A & B setting.

It is certainly not easy to understand why you need an empty space on the card for repeatable mirror image motifs, but not for a single mirror image repeat, except that in the latter case, space is not at a premium. A single repeat can be placed anywhere, and each motif in the single pair can be up to 60sts wide (double if No.3 button used).

Program for the little fishes (Button 2 up).

```
    142                    A motif - Y100,Y1 (FNP), G100
21        60                         B motif - 21 - 60
    121                    B motif - Y100,G34 (FNP), G100
```

Remember, the pattern selector stays in the middle position for all exercises in this section.

The choice of G34 as the FNP for the B motif was arrived at by trial and error. I tried G21 first of all, and the tails were glued together! The more you can visualise the needle plan, the more accurate you will be. Now try the little horses under the dragons on the swatch, and work out the positions yourself. The patterns were centralised, and so you will have similar plottings in the Y as well as in the G part of the bed.

This machine with its unfamiliar pattern plottings can be very frightening to read about, but it is a fascinating and challenging knitting partner with a mind and a personality all of its own.

Little Fishes: Repeatable Mirror Image 910

House & Tree: A & B Motifs 910

Swan & Cygnets: A & B motifs 910

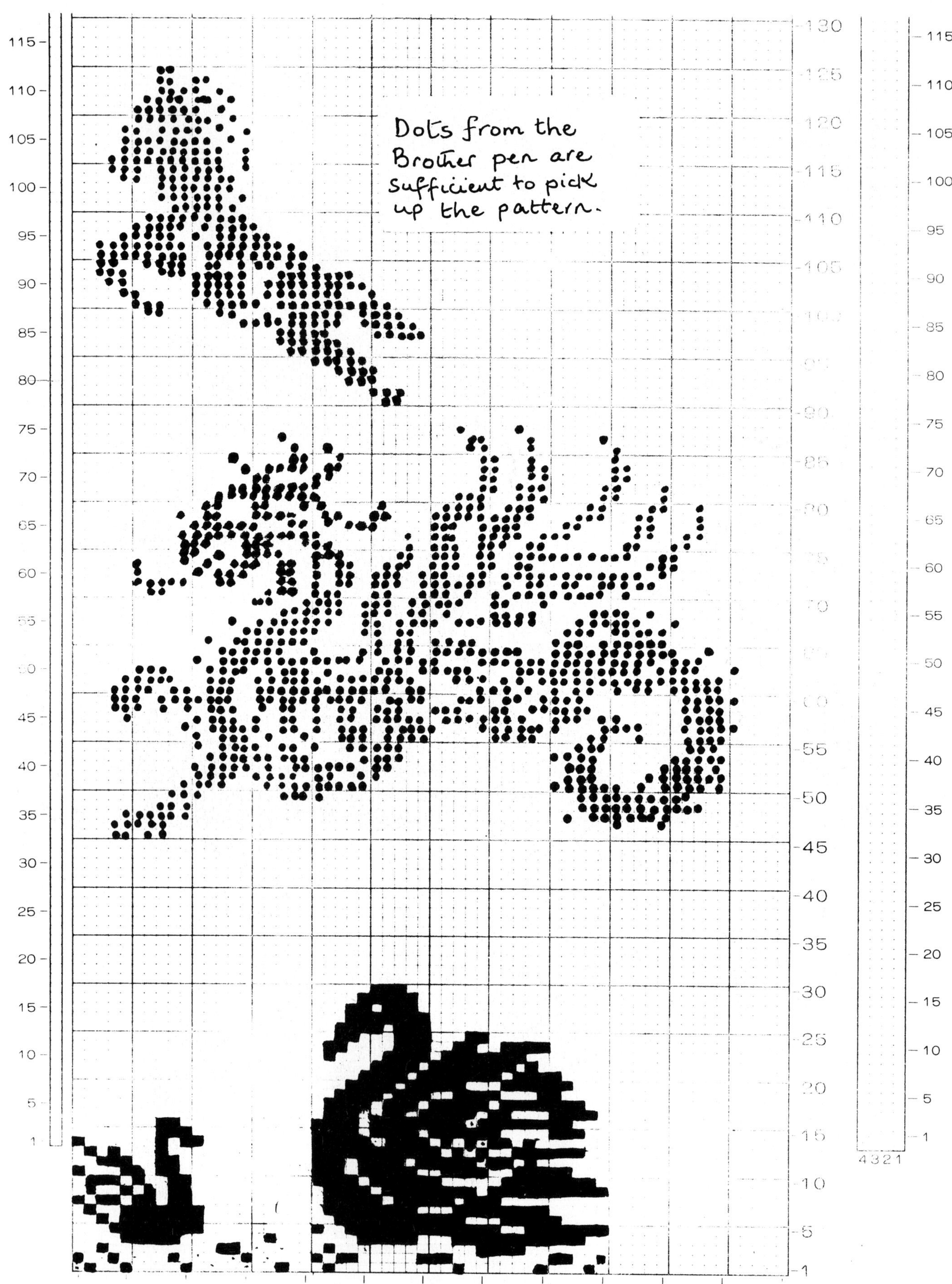

Pattern for Swan & Cygnets

Large Swatch: Animal Motifs 560

Little horses: No.2 button LH light, N.1.C. centre, button 5. Dragons, birds, butterflies: as above but No.2 RH light

c) Picture style motifs.

Though a whole host of pattern combinations are possible, it is the picture style motifs that are so delightful. In RB1 I had the swan and cygnets on two separate punchcards, and promised that one day I would knit them both together in a large repeat system. I had no idea in 1979 what versatility would be possible just five years on, and what meaning one could give to a knitted portrayal such as this.

How do I group motifs on a card?

Either back to back or face to face offers a greater number of options. One could have a completely contrasting pose to the other for the maximum effect.

Knitmaster 500-560. Mark the swan and the two cygnets (all facing left) on the card. Button 2 LH light and button 5 Mirror image. On the needlebed, arrange for the swan and two cygnets at the right, N.1.C. under right PC. At the left, 9sts away, have the second set of PCs a cygnet distance apart. Put the N.1.C. under the left PC. For the second program, shift the main arrangement (swan and two cygnets) to the left of centre, N.1.C. under right PC. As near as possible to the PC at the right, place the left PC of the second arrangement. Place the corresponding right PC with the N.1.C. under it, a cygnet distance away.The third cygnet will be trailing a little, but that adds poignancy to the situation!

At least you have adapted this little picture story to your own system and have reproduced it more or less exactly. You can do the same for a great deal given here for the 910.

NB. Always remove the second set of PCs and N.1.C. from the machine when you have finished with them, and of course, switch off the mirror image, button 5.

To return to the 910 program.

Program 1	Motif A - The swan and facing cygnet Motif B - The cygnet (turned round) repeated twice
Program 2	Motif A - The swan Motif B - The cygnet (turned round) repeated three times.

Plottings for Program 1.

30	A motif - Y38,Y38 (FNP), G7
1 45	B motif - 1 - 15
1	B motif - G8,G8 (FNP), G38 second button up

Plottings for Program 2.

```
   30            A motif - Y33,Y33 (FNP), Y9
21    45                   B motif - 1 - 14
    1            B motif - Y8,G34 (FNP), G34
                           second button up
```

d) Diagonals: overlap, mirror and reflection images.(910,500-560)

On p.72 of the Brother Variation Patterns, and indeed in the Lace pack Vol.2, there are some interesting applications for the diagonal line in Fair Isle and lace. Tuck also offers attractive possibilities (see Book list). As always, let's try to understand why.

Brother 910

1) You can have 2 needle positions side by side (Y1,G1) because though there are an odd number of stitches between the widest points of a chevron (zig-zag) or diamond, the two positions are forced together at the overlapping points of their diagonals. Therefore, we learn that one assumes the dominance. All indications are that it is motif A (more evidence later)

2) The use of No.5 button (Knitmaster Card 1(1) method) ensures that the diagonal travels back to a summit immediately above or below its starting point in the opposite direction. Have the B motif, No.2 button up, if you wish to make a diamond. There are all kinds of permutations and a few are illustrated in the photos. For both Brother and Knitmaster owners, for the lace exercise I have selected one simple diagonal in one of the lace patterns that come with their machines.

Knitmaster 560

Select L15 from your pack. Use mirror image button 5. Mark rows 42 - 50 (width 11sts) for the Card 1(1) method, but first blot out the buzzer and quick return markings with three pieces of sticky tape. An attractive lace diamond is the result.

Horizontal chevron - mark the same pattern for normal return.

Upturned chevron - mark the pattern for method 3 for a quick return to the top.

Now try with the widther at 5. These laces are very easy and quick to do. Although there are 2sts separating the diamonds, the Knitmaster simple lace method produces beautiful, evenly balanced lace patterns. Don't forget to rub out the marks and remove the sticky blobs with a pair of tweezers when you have finished.
NB. The machine reads the special mylar cards that accompany it at a different rate than it reads a pattern you mark on a blank mylar sheet. I only learned that it did when I had done this exercise successfully. Since then I have had a failure, so it is best if you trace off the pattern on to a blank part of a sheet. It doesn't take up much room.

Brother 910.

Take Pattern 10 - 33 from your pack. We select one diagonal, making sure that there is sufficient empty space on the card for its mirror image. The pattern selector is of course in the middle position.

Plottings for Horizontal Chevron.

8	A motif - Y100,Y1 (FNP), G100
18 25	B motif- 18 - 25
1	B motif - Y100,G1 (FNP), G100 second button up

For the Diamond, put button 5 up.

Just a re-cap. We can program an overall pattern with the pattern selector in the middle as well as in the upper and lower positions. In the middle and upper positions, we choose the FNPs. In the bottom one, the machine chooses to centre all patterns on G1.

Incidentally, the Brother patterns are overlapped. Note the difference in the lace holes. The faggot holes occur when the stitches are transferred in the line of the diagonal. The heavier eyelets are formed when the stitches are transferred against the line of the diagonal. If the lace holes alternated on different rows to follow the line then the balance would be restored.

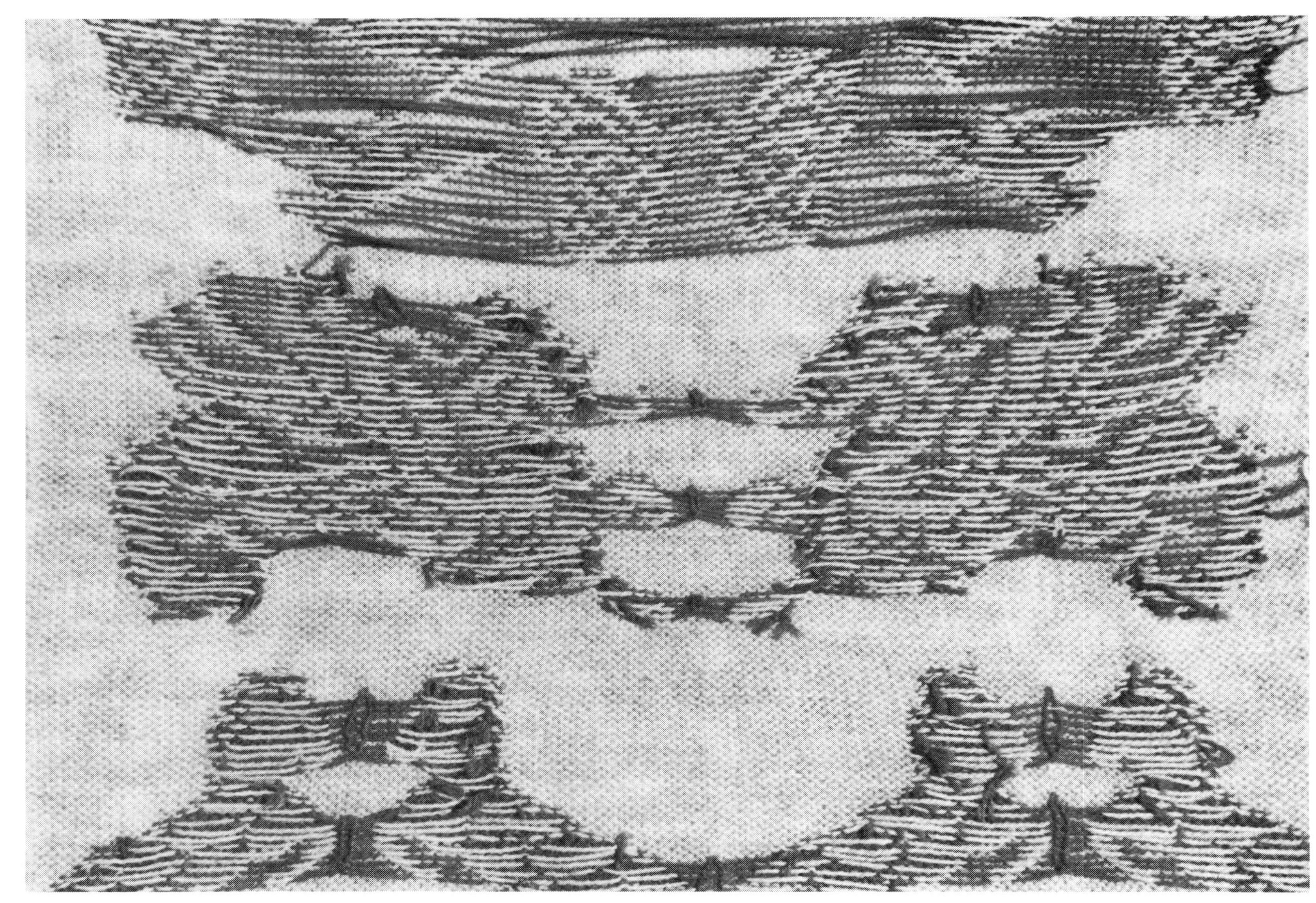

Reverse Side of Animal Motif Swatch
showing cut, knotted and crocheted floats

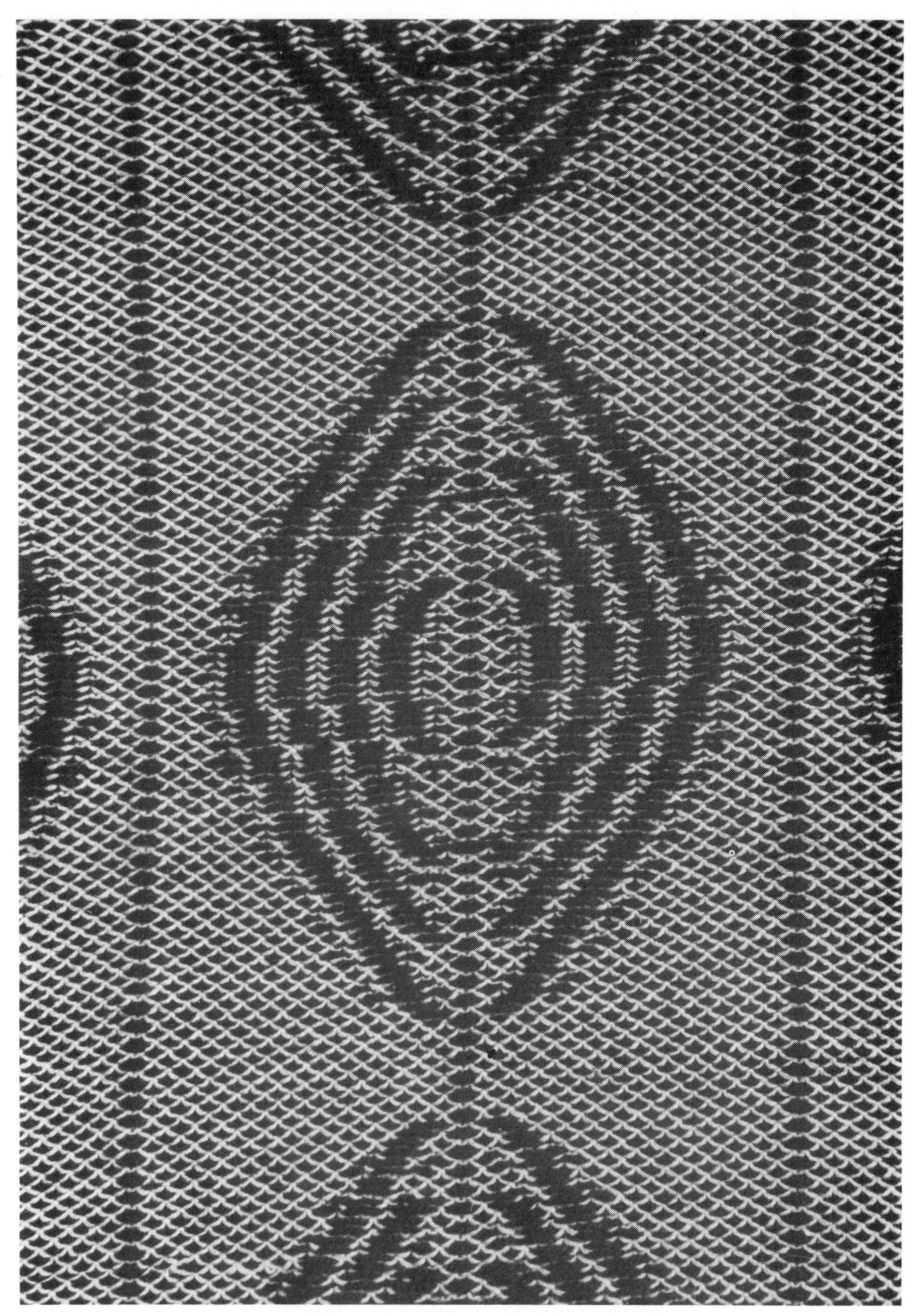

Oval Knitweave Pattern 560

Lace Diagonals 560

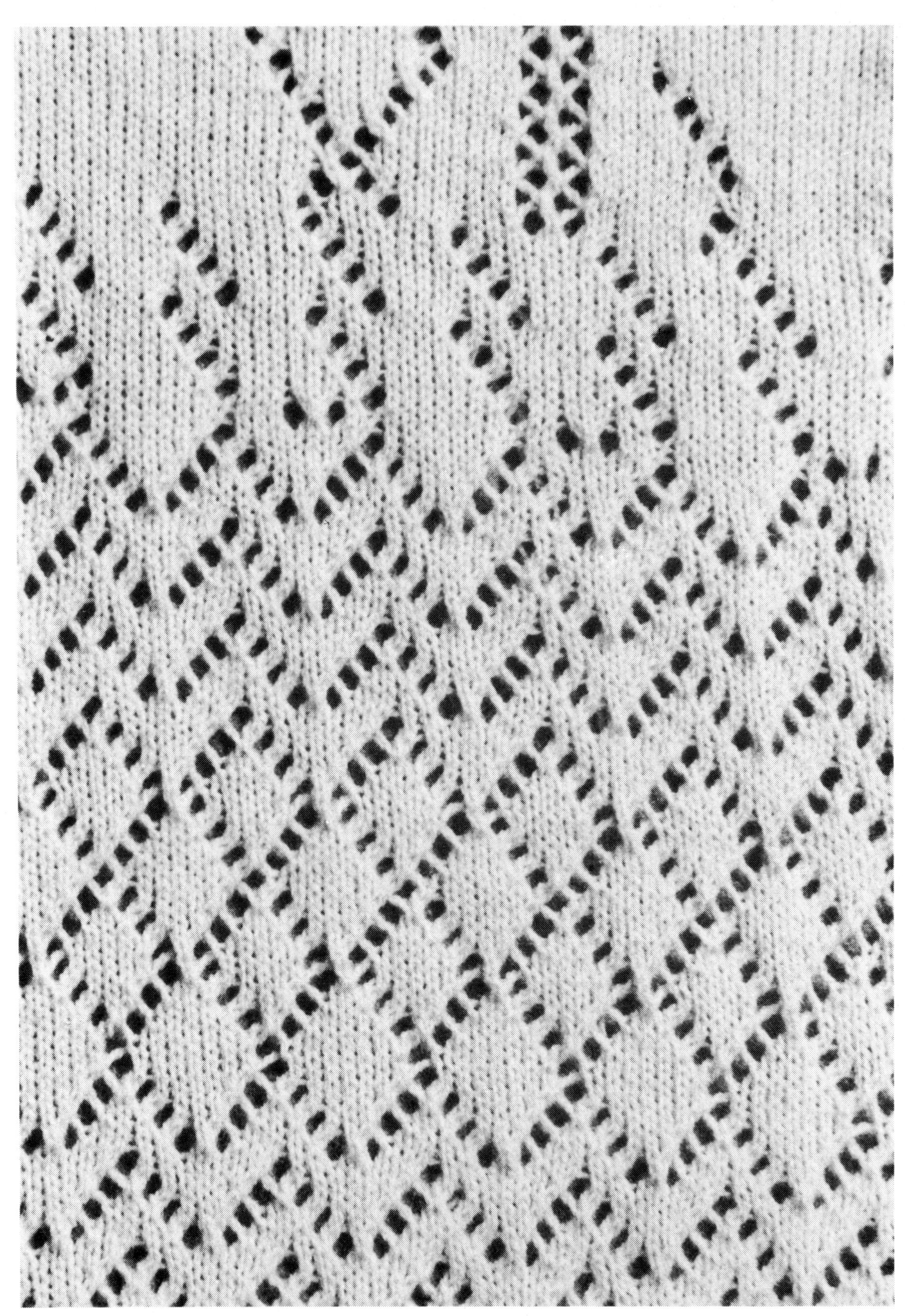

Lace Diagonals 910

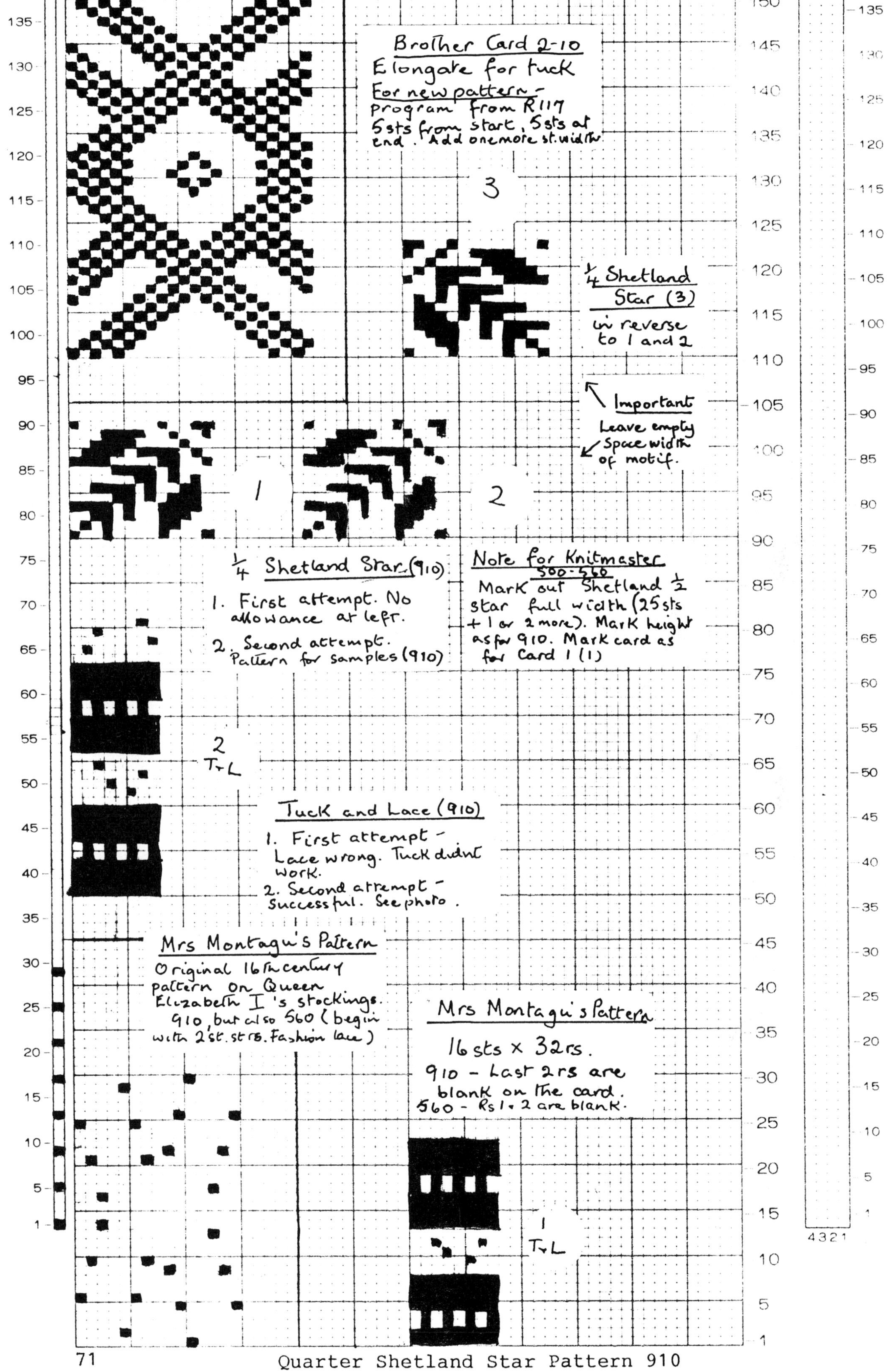

Quarter Shetland Star Pattern 910

Shetland Star: 2 positions

Shetland Star: Tessellated

e) Overall Patterning from a Quarter Image(910).

"How do we get a full size motif and an overall pattern from a quarter size Shetland star?"

The phone rang, and a voice from the Adult Education College in Lerwick asked the question. I knew it was possible with a symmetrical motif. I even knew what methods to employ, but how did I get the right permutation? In actual fact there are several. Two days, and yards of knitting later, I got one answer to send back to Shetland, but not without a helping hand from Jackie Marklew of Jones + Brother. Since then, I have done the reverse quarter successfully (also on the sheet). For this pattern we employ:-

1) horizontal mirror image (so there must be sufficient empty space at the centre side of the motif).

2) overlap of A & B motifs to get the pivot stitch at the centre (A & B are one and the same motif)

3) reflection or vertical mirror image (button 5).

Explanation.

The motif is 25sts wide (12, 1 pivot st. 12). Y1 is FNP. Motif A is in the Y part of the bed, beginning at Y1. Motif B is the one that begins at G1. The actual overlap takes place half a pattern width away from the FNP, as the machine allocates 13sts + 13sts to 25 places. If you want to shift the design as I did, then you shift it to the position of the overlap stitch for the best effect, i.e. 13th or 14th stitch depending on whether you have no stitches between motifs or two.

I tried in vain to get one stitch between motifs until the penny dropped that I was dealing with an exact replica mirror image. You can try it, but you will get a scrambled pattern, as I did many times.

I had two blank rows at the beginning (stocking stitch at KCII). I removed the rows when I wanted the continuous tessellated pattern (1st program, but begin at 91, not 89).

There is no doubt that this quarter image pattern is a boon to commercial knitters. It is very speedy to mark, and requires a small space on the card compared to a full size design, but of course, there must be an equivalent horizontal empty space beside it. Thanks are due to the unknown Shetland lady who asked the question and to Jackie for her help.

For more on a similar, but not identical, type of pattern, see the book Variation Patterns pp.62, 68 & 80. Now try the oval knitweave pattern given here, using the quarter size image to work out your overall pattern. Check that the 1 x 1 background pattern is correct before you knit.

Shetland Star: Plotting the Space

For one space between motifs in a repeatable pattern (500, 560, 910).

Plot half the motif on the sheet plus one space at the side, as we have already done for the Knitmaster machines. Remember to include the top pivot line which is not repeated twice. Brother, use No.5 button and pattern selector down for a straightforward overall pattern, or at the top if you wish to choose your own FNP.

Postscript on overlaps and FNPs.

From what we have learned from lace diagonals and now from the Shetland star, two rules seem to be emerging.

1) Where a pattern has an even number of stitches, i.e. diagonal starting point plus the odd number of stitches in between, then the FNPs are SIDE BY SIDE.

There are two points of overlap on each diagonal to form a diamond.

2) Where a pattern repeat has to have an odd number of stitches created from a half width image that would normally double to an even number, i.e. one more, then the FNPs are

THE SAME e.g. Shetland stars.
There is only one point of overlap.
In both, the overlap forces the dominance of one motif, namely A.

Shetland Star.

Program 1   No space between motifs.

```
    103              A motif - Y100,G1 (FNP), G100
22       46                    B motif - 22 - 46
     89              B motif - Y100,G1 (FNP),G100
```

Program 2   Two stitches between motifs.

```
    103              A motif - Y100,G1 (FNP), G100
21       47                    B motif - 21 - 47
     89              B motif - Y100,G1 (FNP), G100
```

Pattern notes for both programs.
Nos.1 & 5 buttons up. Pattern selector, middle. Leave the appropriate space on the card on both sides of the motif. The pattern actually starts on row 91 after the two blank rows. Now try the reverse image for the star. Better still, go to a 27 or 29 stitch wide symmetrical motif. NB. Use KCI for Fair Isle. Change to KCII for any stocking stitch rows included in the pattern.

f) Superimposition. 910

We have already looked at overlap (see a) Basic Representations). In Variation Patterns p.74, a solid diamond overlaps a diamond outline to create a new repeatable pattern in F.I. Try the same idea, only this time put a diagonal line besides the solid diamond and program both so that the diamond is superimposed over diagonal stripes. The combined pattern area is still under Fair Isle.

In this section, we are concerned with the superimposition of solid stocking stitch shapes over lace, Fair Isle, weaving and tuck. There is nothing about this kind of superimposition in any manual. Anne Bayes once said that as ideas float above the world they are plucked out of the air simultaneously. We could say that knitters beam in on a common wavelength.
About the same time as the Australians were working with Yuki Mitsumata of Brother on the following filet-type lace pattern, the Auckland 910 club in New Zealand came up with the same method quite independently.

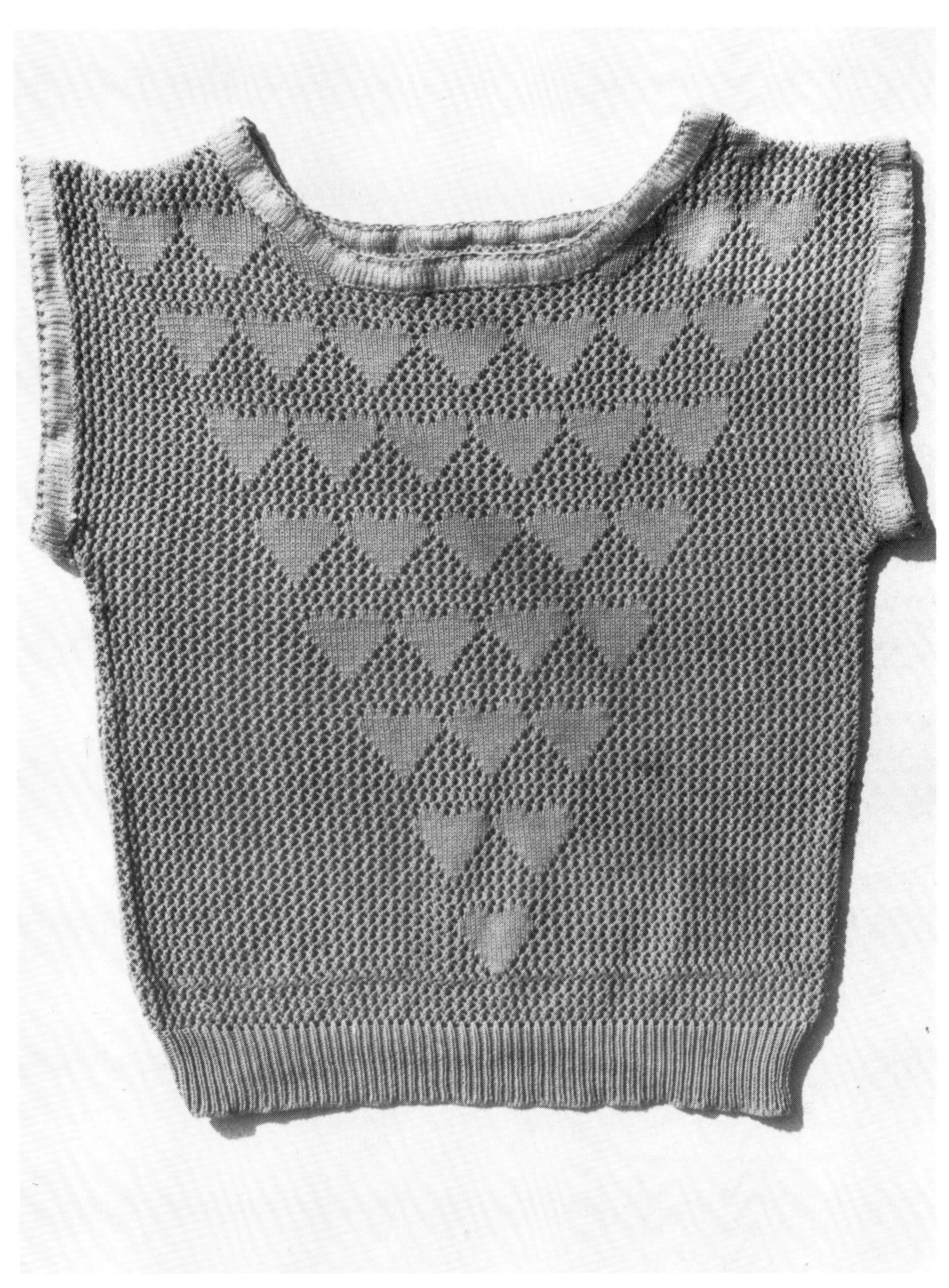

Filet Lace Sweater 910

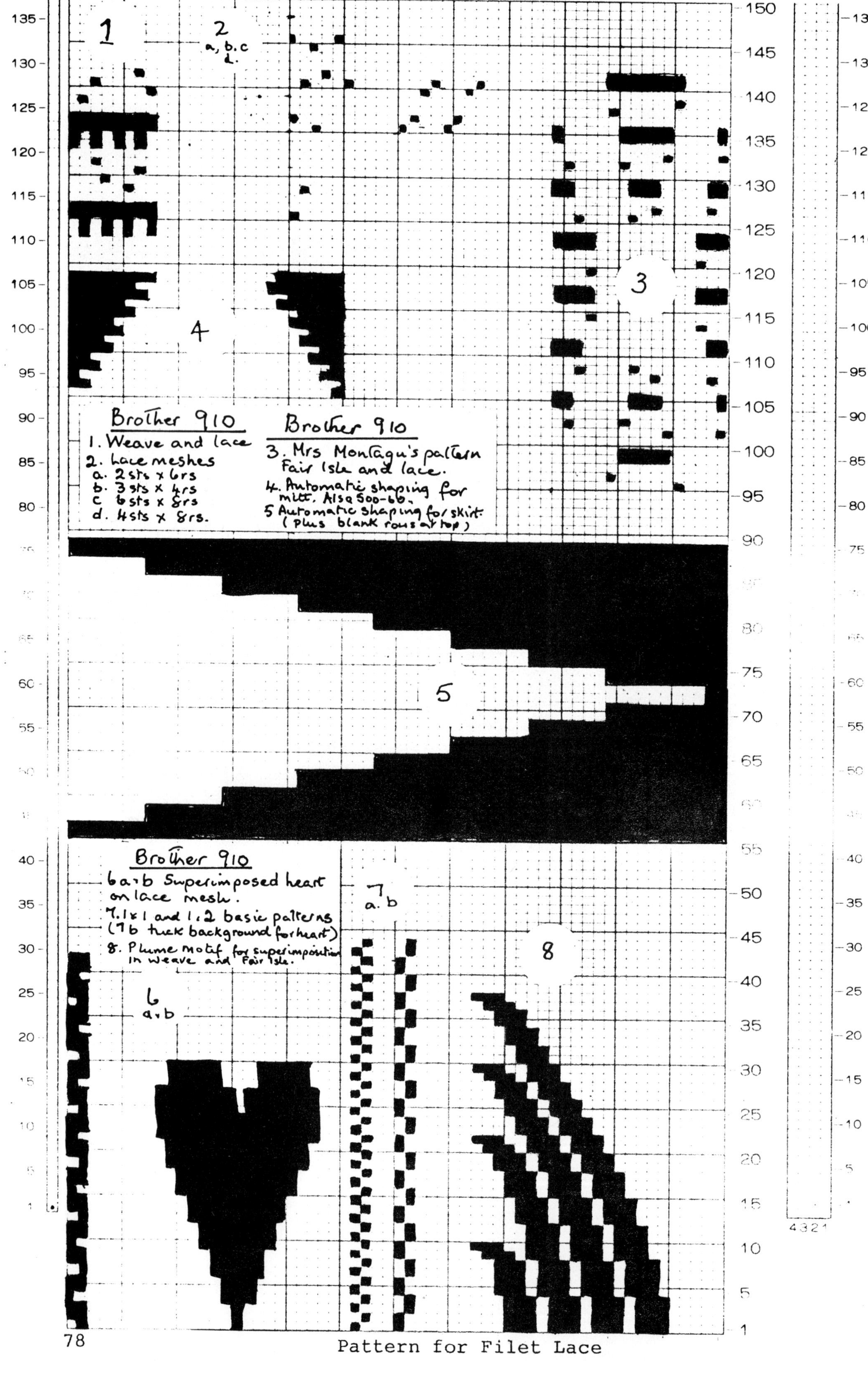

Pattern for Filet Lace

Yuki's Pattern: Filet Lace (courtesy Brother)

42
1 2
1

A motif - Y100,G1 (FNP), G100
Pattern selector-middle,
No.6 button up

A motif program constant throughout. Add more motifs if desired.

Program 1
B motif - 9-23
Y7,Y7 (FNP), G8

Program 2
B motif - 9-24
Y15,Y15 (FNP),G16

Program 3
B motif - 9-24
Y23,Y7 (FNP),G24

Program 4
B motif - 9-24
Y31,Y15 (FNP),G32

Program 5
B motif - 9-24
Y39,Y7, (FNP),Y40

Program 6
B motif - 9-24
Y47,Y15 (FNP), G48

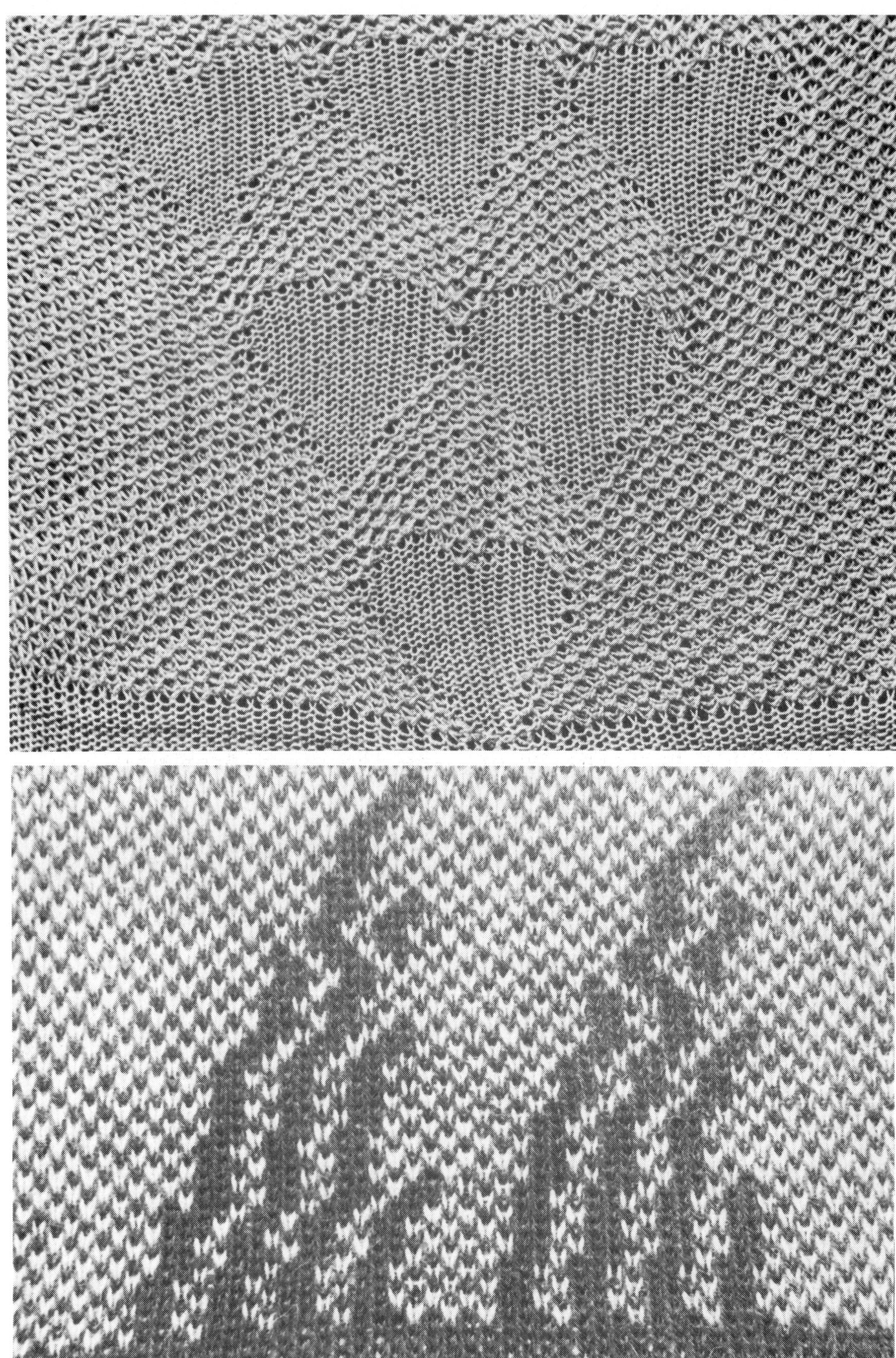

Heart over Tuck; Fair Isle Plume 910

Plume Knitweave 560

Their experiments were published first in the N.Z.M.K.S. Festival Handbook, and then sent to Alles Hutchinson's News and Views, U.S.A. Yuki's pattern was sent to me very kindly by Anne Bayes and I immediately adapted and knitted it on a cap sleeved top for myself, jotting down any notes and explanations I felt could be useful to as many 910 knitters as possible (courtesy of Brother).

1) Basic Principle of Filet Lace

What we have to understand is that the machine cannot program stocking stitch as a pattern unless the No.6 button is up and the stocking stitch pattern shape is blacked in on the card. The needles stay back at B, as in tuck, and the selection is reversed for, say, a pattern like Fair Isle. The lace stitch also has to have reverse pattern markings. The blanks in the lace section are the selected needles.
NOTE. The N.Z. knitters called this type of pattern filet lace because it reminded them of real filet lace, where isolated solid patterns are worked in a background of mesh by the lacemaker.

2) Program for Filet Lace (A & B motif)

This is a complete overlap. The basic faggot lace mesh is the A motif, and the stocking stitch heart pattern is the B. We begin with the program marked A for one single motif (see p.78). Notice that we choose the FNP as G1, and that we program the full width of the bed. To stop the end needles selecting i.e. in from the edge, use orange L cams or just push the needles back. Programming this as well would be too complicated.

The width of the B motif is 15sts in the first program (9-23), but in every other one it is 16sts i.e. 15sts + 1 stitch to separate the motifs.

When you have knitted the first program, the beeper goes and the card returns to half a tiny grid below the 1 mark in the L window. STOP.

In this pattern, the lace repeat is continuous, so you can re-program as soon as the card returns **one row earlier** than normal. Why? Here we are dealing with lace, and that's the difference. The last row on the card is actually the selecting row for the first row of the next sequence, and we don't need that here. Notice how the machine treats a new program. The card does not move on the first row until there is selection. A new program cancels the old memory, and the machine begins again.

3) Multiples of B motifs

To understand how to offset and place, notice the pattern sequences of the FNPs, 7, 15, 7, 15, and so on. There is a difference of 8 between each number marking the limits of the pattern within the yellow and green needle sections (Pattern width 15 + 1). Each group of patterns is shifted half a width out at each side, thereby adding one whole pattern in the process.

Knitmaster: the lace inversion method on the 560 is efficient and speedy with the aid of the PCs. This is your equivalent to filet lace, unless you do two consecutive overall patterns, one for mesh and one for solid on mesh. Try the heart pattern in this book. The principle governing the movement of the PCs is the same. Move them out half a pattern width after one whole pattern in rows has been knitted (see 560 manual, p.46 Sectional Knitting)

Knitmaster and Brother: once you have understood how to increase the pattern area, you can add as many rows of motifs as you choose, as I did to suit my own size.

4) Why are there three knit stitches in the first row of the first pattern?

The lowest point of the stocking stitch heart rests on one stitch, as per pattern card. It is in a base of 1 x 1 faggot lace mesh, and it so happens that the B motif is superimposed over a selected stitch flanked by a knit stitch on both sides, making three stitches in all. The three stitches occur in every alternate grouping of B motifs. It is an indication that one can never be entirely sure of the precise shape of the B motif in superimposition until one has tested it.

Sweater showing lace inversion and filet lace:

exclusive design by Denise Musk (910)

5) How do you program a few rows of overall lace mesh?

I found out the hard way. I began with 16rs and programmed an overall lace mesh (Pattern selector down), and couldn't understand for long enough why there was a mispattern when I began the A & B pattern. Then I understood. Reason: pattern switch down means that the pattern is always centred on G1, but in the programs for the superimposition (Pattern switch, middle position), the FNP is G1, and that is not the same thing at all. In the first case, G1 didn't select, being the second stitch of the pattern repeat.In the second case it did, being the first stitch of the pattern repeat. There is a choice of alternatives, using the switch in the top position.

1) Program the position on the card and EXACTLY the same position on the bed as for motif A in the superimposition, Y100, G1 (FNP), G100.

2) Since 2 is the pattern base, and a factor of 100, program the FNP as Y100. The first stitch in the repeat after the central 0 will then be G1.

You will find that you don't need to re-program the whole of the pattern every time. Run it through quickly with your finger on the M button, stopping only to input new data (MKI & II).

6) How do you divide for the neck?

I prefer the method whereby I note the row number in the L window at the point of division.

When I returned to knit the left side, the RR button was pressed, the row number programmed, and the CF button pushed. The card advanced to the correct spot. Here, however, we had a problem. The B motif pattern I had finished with at the right top shoulder was not the same one I'd left at the centre neck. Therefore, I went back to the previous program and put it into the machine. I followed the procedure correctly, and the pattern was wrong and continued to be wrong after several attempts. I blamed the sun, and the customers in the shop blamed the sun, which was indeed shining on the machine. Then it occurred to me that both FNPs were no longer operative in the WP needle setup for the left neck side, though that should not have mattered at all. I devised a new program for A & B motifs contained within the WP needles. It worked; the pattern was correct, and the sun was still shining. Later I succeeded in what I failed to do earlier, and I am tempted to describe the experience as a mystery. Note: the back was knitted in allover faggot lace mesh.

Superimposition: weave on weave; stocking stitch on 1 x 1 Fair Isle.

For the weaving pattern and the F.I., I chose the plume pattern as the B motif superimposed over an A motif of 1 x 1 selection. With both I realised as I was knitting that the A motif was too powerful, and was destroying the delicacy of the plume curve. The B motif should have been much bolder and stronger in shape, or I could have reversed the patterns.

On some rows, there was hardly any selection across the plume motif area, and then I started to select with my fingers. Instead of describing these attempts as disasters, I am excited by the free style design possibilities that can be explored over a repeatable pattern of this kind.

Superimposition: stocking stitch hearts over 1 x 2 tuck.

This was much more of a success. I used 2 x 2/24 bright courtelle (plated), and the effect was very interesting. Obviously, the heart shape exerted much more influence on the 1 x 2 tuck than the waving plumes did on a background of 1 x 1. NB. No.6 button must be down, the blanks on the 1 x 2 pattern represent tucks. Use the program for the hearts in the filet lace pattern.

g) Automatic shaping using slip (part).

This is an automatic electronic version of the Passap BX with pushers holding position method of shaping. The needles held remain at B position, and in skirt patterns the resting needles nearest to the carriage need to be wrapped. On the raglan and mitt patterns, the tooth edged manner of marking ensures a self wrap as the carriage returns. Compare with the example given for a lacy raglan, where the stitches are not wrapped. You would crochet, figure of 8, or knit the sleeve downwards to seal the seams in the latter example.

ONLY STOCKING STITCH can be used, though one can incorporate patterns in the area outside of that governed by the pattern card (mitts and skirts in particular). There is a lot of marking to be done on the card. The Brother pen is probably the best to use here. Though a dot is normally sufficient to convey a pattern message to the machine, it is more appropriate in this instance to fill the squares entirely. Incidentally, ordinary drawing inks do not seem to work. You need special inks like the Staedtler 747 (not 745), or the Rotring TT ink, procured from office suppliers.

detail from quilt "Summer Meadow"

(mirror image - jacquard)

"Winter Trees" - sculptured lace

"Birds in Lace"

exclusive designs by Patricia Lacey (910) Photos: J.A.Lacey

Programs & Sketch for Raglan 910

Size 61cm

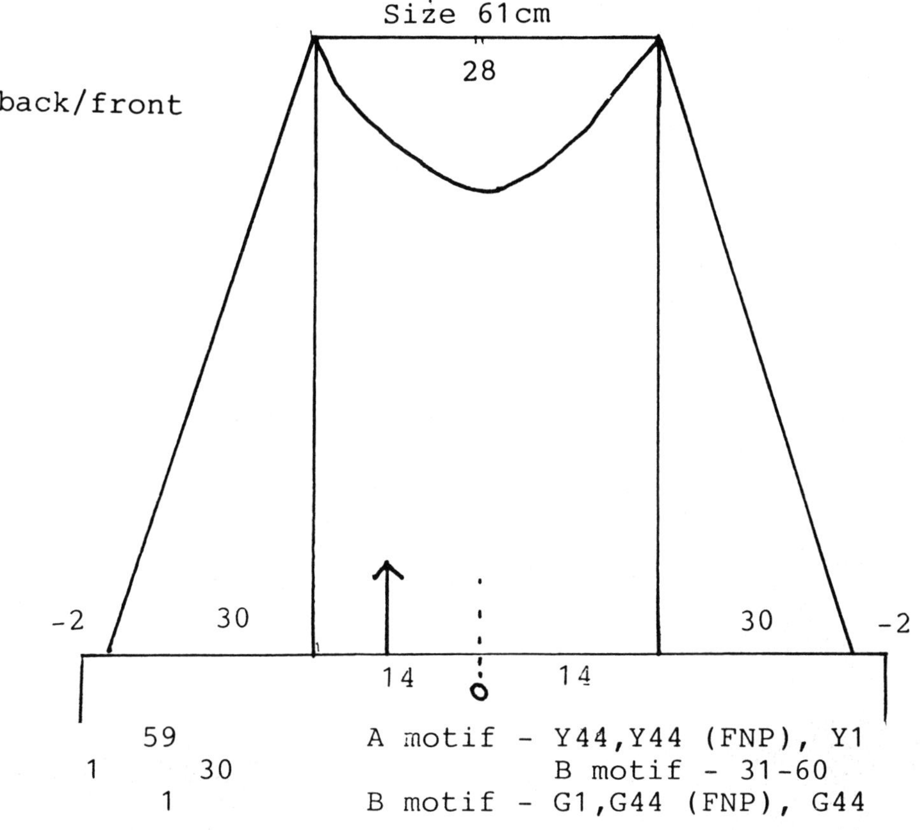

59 A motif - Y44,Y44 (FNP), Y1

1 30 B motif - 31-60

1 B motif - G1,G44 (FNP), G44

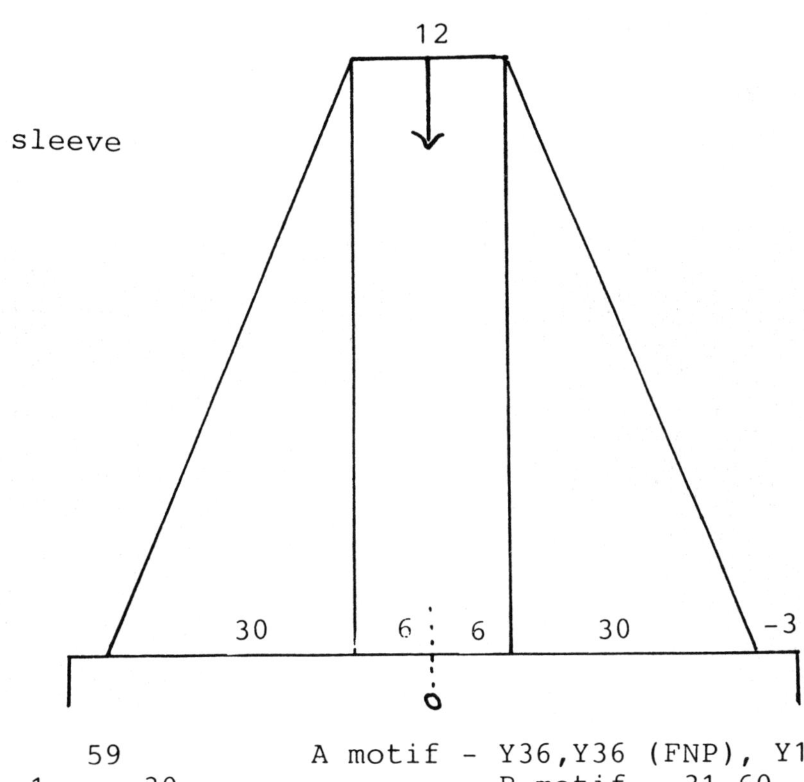

59 A motif - Y36,Y36 (FNP), Y1

1 30 B motif - 31-60

1 B motif - G1,G36 (FNP), G36

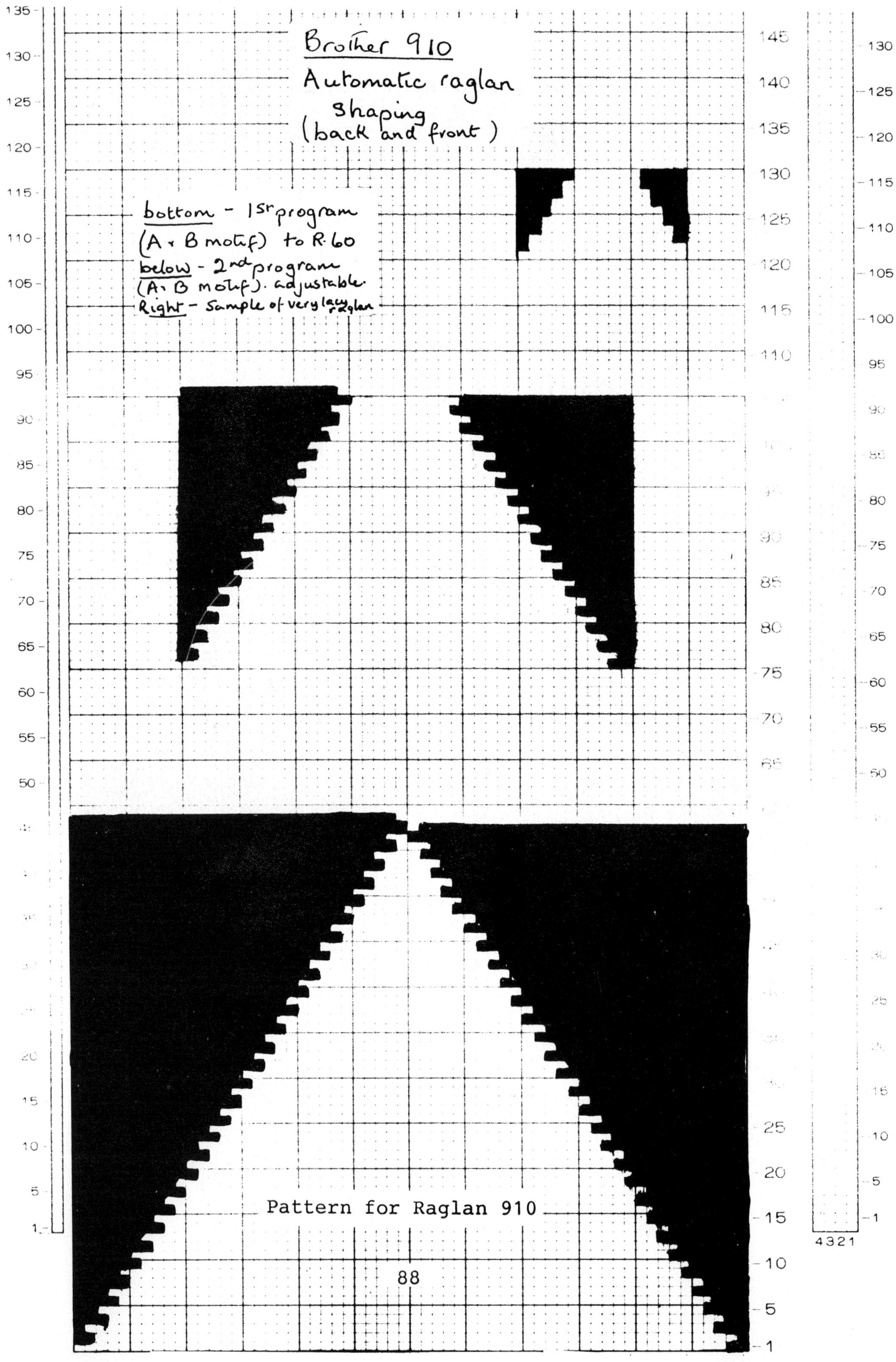
Brother 910
Automatic raglan shaping (back and front)
bottom - 1st program (A + B motif) to R.60
below - 2nd program (A + B motif). adjustable.
Right - sample of very lacy raglan
Pattern for Raglan 910
4321

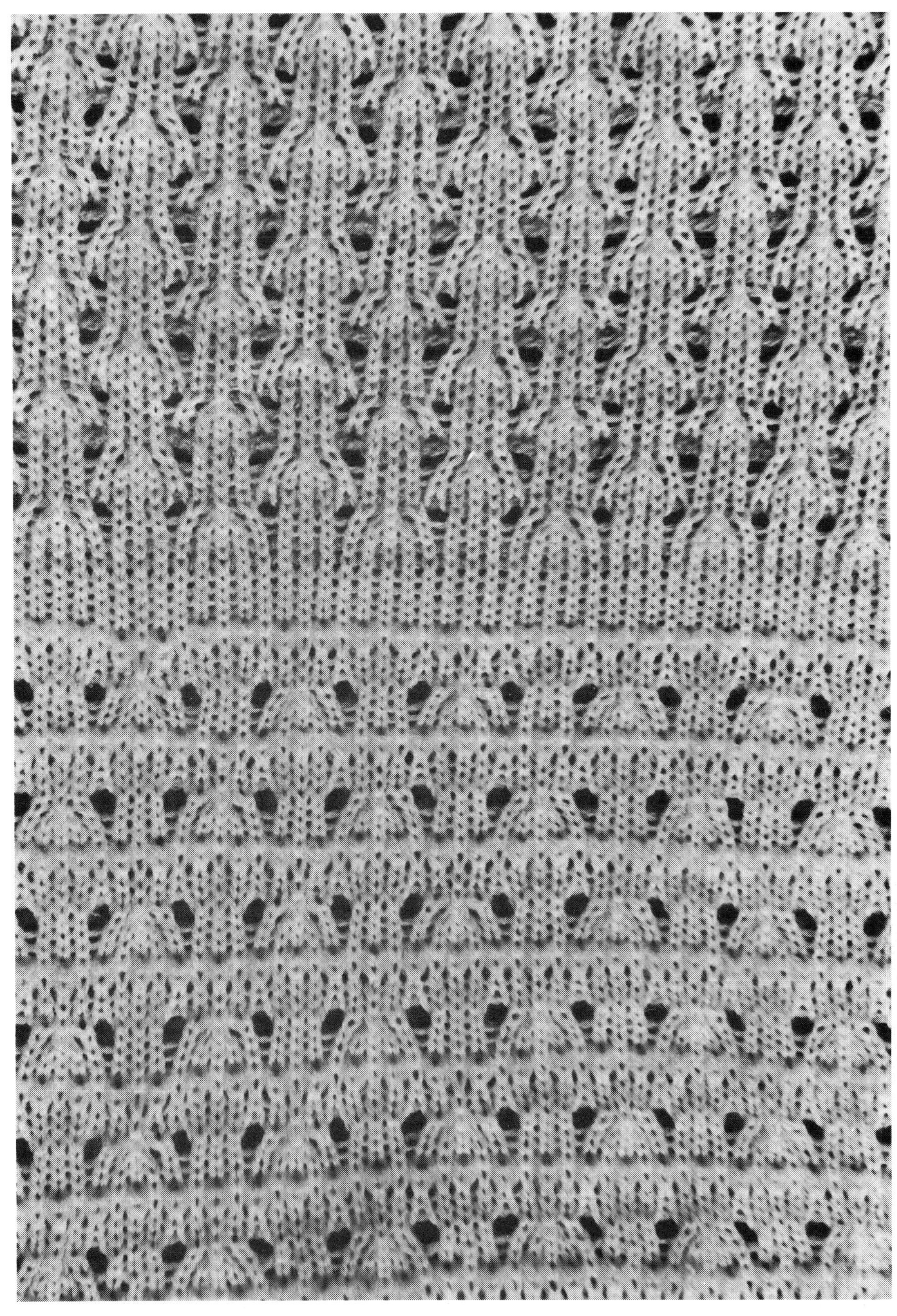

Tuck & Lace, Weave & Lace: Knitside 910

Fair Isle & Lace 910   Mrs Montagu's Pattern

One must weigh the time taken for marking against shaping by the normal method, and must also bear in mind that the markings only relate to one yarn and its stitch and row tension, in my case, 4 ply, in the standard 28sts - 40rs per 10cms, as well as to one particular pattern style. On the other hand, if one requires standard-type stocking stitch darts, necklines, shoulders, all-in-one raglans, mitts, socks and sideways knitted skirts on a regular basis, then the effort is worth it. For skirts, it most certainly is. In any case, the exercises are very interesting and the method of knitting, most speedy.

There are two methods of marking the card and programming the machine.

1) Button 6 up - the black area on the card represents slipped or held stitches. The blank, unmarked area represents stocking stitch knitting (mitts, raglans and socks).

2) Button 6 down - the black area on the card represents stocking stitch knitting, and the blank, unmarked area, stitches slipped or held (skirts).

NB. Use KCII for both 1 & 2.

Note for Knitmaster 500-560.

Shaping for mitts and socks can be plotted on your mylar card. In the case of method 1, the No.1 button, right hand light is on.

Note for Brother and Knitmaster.

Only half the circumference of socks and mitts needs to be marked and only half the shaping, since we use the Card 1(1) method of marking (Knitmaster), and No.5 button up (Brother). This is most interesting to do, and the heel, toe or top of the mitt is shaped in no time at all. I have plotted on the card the shaping for the mitt pattern in RB2 p.69, third size.

The A & B motif - how does it work?

a) Skirts (910).

Knitters find the pattern markings most intriguing. The No.3 (horizontal expansion) button up, and No.6 button down. I have drawn an adaptation of the skirt pattern in RB2. I should have left space above the marked wedge for the knit rows between shaped gores. If the wedge is 30rs you leave 30 spaces. Should you choose to do a pattern here then you mark it. If you prefer to insert half of the straight wedge of knitting in the middle of the shaping, then pull the marked gore apart, and leave the correct even number of blanks. Release part buttons for this and knit stocking stitch, still on KCII.

You must understand that what you see on the card does not represent the whole of the skirt length i.e. widthways, sideways knitted. To the left, the marked area graduates to blank. On the bed of the machine, this represents the waist area. ALL NEEDLES TO THE LEFT OF THIS NOT REPRESENTED ON THE CARD WILL SLIP.

On the card, your A motif width is from 1 - 58. Your B motif width is 59 - 60 (solid black i.e. knitting stitches).ALL NEEDLES TO THE RIGHT OF THIS NOT REPRESENTED ON THE CARD WILL KNIT. This is the bottom edge of the skirt, 7 marks = 14sts held. Program to G100 max. Don't forget to lay the yarn in the needle head of the resting needle nearest the carriage. The height of the motif must include the blank rows which I have omitted. The choice here is yours. Do try the pattern to understand the technique, and then you will soon adapt your own favourite skirt pattern for this very speedy method (see book list). NB. There is no need to have 14sts every time. There is one group of 18 nearest the bottom edge of the skirt. You can adjust to suit. The optimum length of the skirt should be between 170 - 184 needles.

Exercise - Sideways knitted A-line skirt- waist 71 (28)cm.

Length 63 (25)cm. Tension 28sts - 40rs per 10cms at T.7 approx.

Copy pattern onto the bottom of a new mylar sheet and include 30rs blank at the top (34 + 30 = 64rs height). Push up into working position 90ns on either side of 0 (180ns). Cast on in WY. Knit 7rs. Carr. at left. Change to MY and MT. Knit 14rs. Carr. at left. Input program (below). Button 3 up, KCII, pattern selector middle, CF. Knit 1r to right for selection.RC000.

*Push in part buttons and knit. At row 34 no further selection will be made within the shaped gore area. Release part buttons, still on KCII ** Knit 30rs stocking stitch. Card returns to R1 on R63 (i.e. R29 of stocking stitch section). Selection is made on R64 *** Repeat from * to *** 9 times in all. Repeat from * to ** once. Knit 15rs stocking stitch (10 shaped gores). Change knob to NL. Change to WY. Knit 7rs. Release from machine.

Tip. Tie a piece of WY on edge stitch at beg. of each shaped gore to make counting easy. Add more gores if you wish. Remember to wrap inner resting ns held at B position.

Note 24sts (10sts for waist hem + 14) at left are not within the pattern area and therefore slip during the shaping of the gore. The 40sts at the right controlled by the B motif will knit. Make up in the usual way. Turn down hems at waist and bottom edge, or else apply crochet to the bottom edge for a longer skirt.

Program

```
    64            A motif - Y66,Y66 (FNP), G50
1      58                  B motif - 59 - 60
     1            B motif - G51,G51 (FNP), G90
```

Allocation of stitches

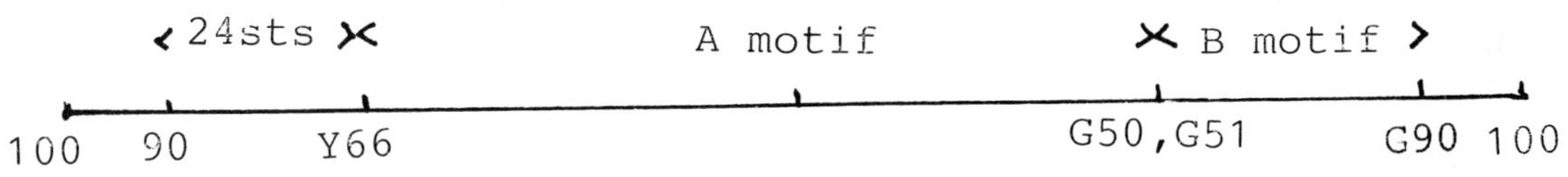

```
    < 24sts ><             A motif            >< B motif >
|------|--------|--------------|------------------|--------|--|
100   90       Y66                       G50,G51        G90 100
```

b) Raglans (910)

We have No.6 button up for this, as the blacked out areas are stitches to be slipped or held. For an adult garment, you will have to have two main programs for back/front and sleeves (4 altog.). What are missing from the first program on the mylar sheet are the stitches you are left with for front and back necks (the sleeve will require its own programs). The stitches in the centre will knit anyway as they are not touched by shaping. Motif A is the left half and motif B is the right. The first program can only be 60rs long, the second one is adjustable according to size. Note: the width is programmed as the shortest side of the right-angled triangle, with the tooth edge as the longest. The space separating them represents the needles that will knit on the bed, not shown in the first program. The width of each of the A & B motifs shown in Program 1 is 30sts. A is one row taller, and so is at the left. The A & B motifs in both the skirt and the raglan are side by side. In the raglan the last WP needle furthest from the centre is both first needle in the setup and FNP, while the one in the middle is Y1 or G1. The sleeve is graft-knitted from top to bottom, No.5 button up.

Exercise: All-in-one Raglan Sweater Size 61 (24)cm. 28sts - 40rs per 10cms.

Mark out the programs A & B in your notebook (see diagrams). Input Program 1. Knit the back and the front of the toddler's sweater from my Resource Book Pattern Supplement p.110, size 61, or choose an equivalent Marion Nelson card, 4 ply. Knit, if you wish, the little horse on the motif sheet instead of the cartoon puppy. An all-in-one raglan is better than a conventionally knitted raglan if you wish the shaping to show. At the underarm set the cam to hold. Cast off 2sts at the right, knit to the left and program the pattern before you cast off the 2sts at the left. No.6 button up, Pattern selector middle. The next row will select. Push in the part buttons and knit. Move claw weights up on WP needles every few rows. Push out the group of edge needles as you get near the top. The knitting on these will drag down as your work proceeds. Knit to row 59. Scrap off the centre stitches left in WP (back), and with two contrasting WYs, scrap off the left and right raglan edges. Knit front same, casting off stitches as required at centre neck.

Sleeve.

Push out 12ns to WP at centre, 6 on either side of 0. Knit a few rows of WY over these, carr. at left. Hitch up back and front stitches on either side of centre 12ns, purl side facing, neck towards middle. Input Program 2, Nos.5 & 6 buttons up. Program row 59 on card. Remove WY on raglan edges. Hang claw weights in middle. Press CF. Change to MY. Knit to right for selection, part buttons in, and continue. You will find the needles re-introduced, and the knitting very speedy indeed.

NB. When you knit an adult's or a large child's size, and you need two separate programs for one piece, be sure to push out to HP all needles directed to rest by the first program. Reason: needles at B, outside those represented by the marked pattern, will knit. It is very important to hang claw weights in the fabric under the WP needles in the middle and move the weights up as you knit.

OVERALL PATTERNING - 3 BROTHER SPECIALITIES

For these three combination stitch patterns, the pattern selector is down. You may well find other methods of marking the card and knitting the patterns. I am only passing on what I have found to be workable, while at the same time I recognise there are alternatives.

1) Weave and lace.

There are no patterns for this or for the other two combination patterns in the 910 manuals, or pre-marked card sets. While we can get inspiration from punchcard pattern books, their pattern markings do not help us. For one carriage following another in the same direction on a punchcard machine, the punchcard only advances one row. On the 910, the magnet on the back of each carriage ensures that the card will move on EVERY TIME a patterning carriage, lace or main, goes across the centre of the bed. Therefore each carriage has its own individual marks on the card. In one way it is easier, but we must remember:

a) the pre-select row

b) the card has to be marked correctly for each of the stitch patterns in the combination

c) the first needle selection, KCI or KCII on the main carriage, the non-first needle selection on the lace carriage. Do we need to push out the first and last needles to D, or push them back to B for the second pattern in the combination?

d) we only use one carriage across the belt at once to avoid damage to the machine.

The easiest way to begin is to do what I did. I used Card 1(1), and knitted myself a sideways knitted suit in lace and weave. I used the lace carriage to make rows of holes to enclose bands of 1 x 1 weave from the same card. In the middle of the pattern, to correct the bias of the holes, I began with the lace carriage at the right for transfer. The procedure is very easy and you don't have to think about the pattern at all. It's as good an introduction as any to the basic effect you are after.

Hint: If you hear a deep groan from the belt, you have two carriages geared into it. The belt is telling you it can't bear the strain. Take off the one you are not using and put it on to the lace rail out of harm's way.

The weave and lace pattern

Look at the Brother 910 mylar sheet with the skirt shaping marked on it. The weave and lace pattern is No.1 at the top left.

143
1 8
124

All buttons down. Please note how the weave pattern is marked on the card. The selected needles are those marked in black, and so for the two stocking stitch rows all needles select. I didn't mark the weave rows or the lace rows in the L window because it was very easy to know when to change. We begin with the main carriage going from left to right, just this once as a starting procedure. Needles select. Weaving brushes down. Lay weaving yarn across for two rows. (I used Bonnie's Mosaic 4ply over Patsy Fine) Knit two more rows (4 altog.) Carr. at right. Use lace carr. for 4 transfers (6rs). Weave 2rs, knit 2rs, and so on.

This is a very pretty, fashioned lace pattern, which looks lovely on the knit side with the delicate print-dyed weaving yarn peeping through the holes.

Alternative method of marking

No.6 button up. This time make the lace marks blanks set in a background of solid black. You can leave the weaving pattern as it is and the stocking stitch rows blank. Which method do you prefer?

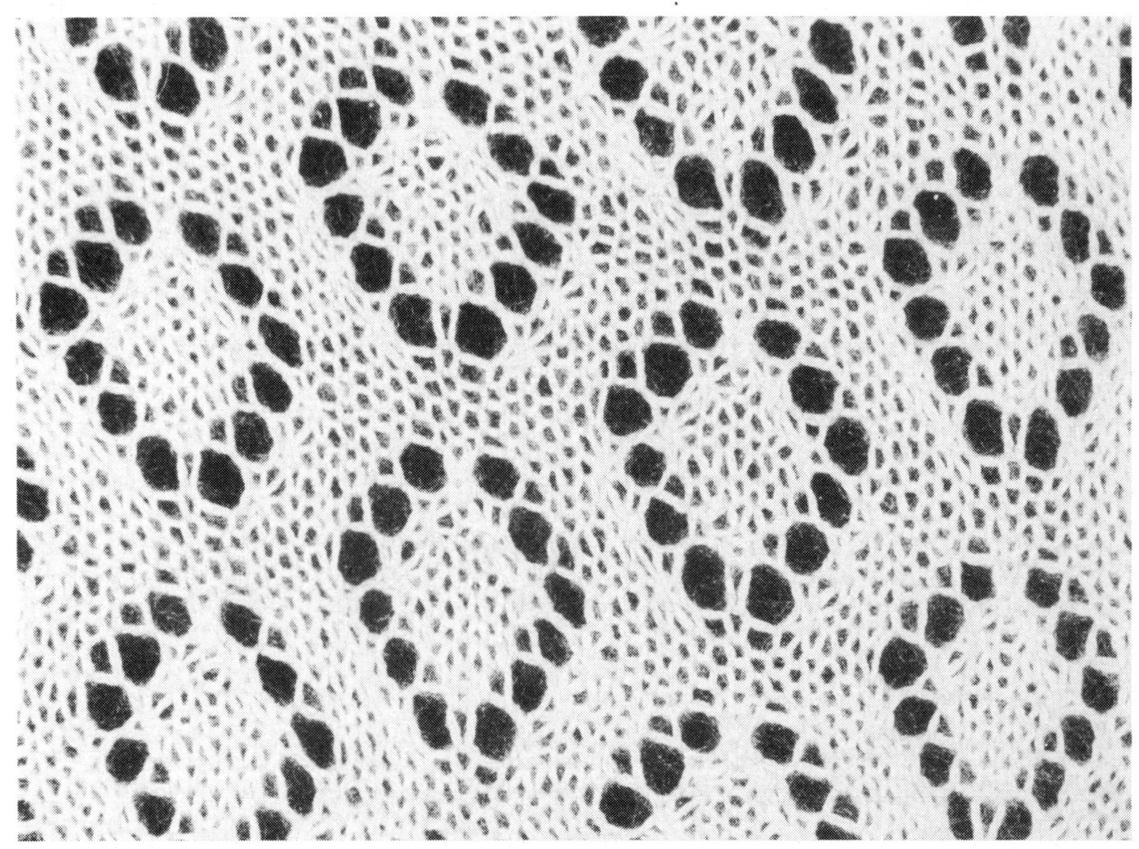

Mrs Montagu's Pattern: the original courtesy B.T.Batsford

2) Tuck and Lace

I used the same lace pattern as No.1 but got into difficulties as you can see. I deliberately left my first effort on the sheet for you to compare (see mylar sheet with quarter Shetland star). The problem here is that the needles must:

a) be suitably selected for tuck stitch

b) have knitted at least one row of stocking stitch for the tuck loops to stay in place (use claw weights on cast-on comb). Again, all buttons are down.

81
1 8
51

Begin with main carriage at right. Push in part buttons and take carr. to left. Select to right. Do this only once. Again, I didn't mark the L window, because the needle selection told me where I was. 4rs stocking stitch, 4rs tuck, 4rs stocking stitch, and so on.

Note: the lace carriage will not select the first and last needles, so push them out by hand for the tuck row. Next time, I shall be more adventurous with my tuck pattern before experimenting with the lace.

3) Fair Isle and Lace

This is a comparatively new combination stitch which we first saw in Nihon Vogue publications and then in the new Toyota Knitting Pattern Book. This one I find very exciting, with lots of possibilities once we have understood how to develop them. I took the famous lace pattern I featured in my book for Batsford, Techniques in Machine Knitting, and wondered how Queen Elizabeth I would have reacted if Mrs Montagu had knitted lace and Fair Isle on those celebrated stockings, now in Hatfield House Museum.

You will find the pattern on the top right of the mylar sheet featuring the skirt shaping. Compare it with the original on the sheet with the Shetland star. Note: we have chosen to have the contrast colour INSIDE the diamond. The choice really is ours, and there are many possibilities. End with a blank row on the card.

143
45 60
96

Start with the lace carriage which, at the end of its run, brings out multiple groups of needles which cannot be mistaken for anything other than Fair Isle selection. The pattern is organised to allow the lace carriage to follow its normal sequence. Always in lace there is a free move row at the beginning of a sequence except for the very first row (once only). This, strangely enough, is the last row of the pattern, and that is why it is blank on the card. Set the main carriage to KCII, and push out the first needle by hand. Knit 2rs Fair Isle between every lace sequence. The result is very beautiful, with the contrast colour etched with lace holes and the coloured strands peeping through.

Note on new blank mylar sheets

These sheets which are now on the market are thinner than the ones we have had previously. What is more, you can easily remove the blue grid lines with a pencil rubber. If this happens, put the sheet EXACTLY over one of the blank graph paper sheets provided, or over another blank mylar card. The grid of the undersheet will provide the guidelines you need for the pattern.

Notes on the Brother 910 MKII

If there is a sticker across p.89 of the instruction manual informing you that there is a modified backup memory but no batteries in the machine, you have a MKII model, which is fitted with a condenser to enable the machine to retain a more complex memory procedure. Jones + Brother say that if the machine has not been used " for a considerable length of time" it would be advisable to leave the machine switched on for at least an hour to charge the condenser up. Incidentally, if you press through the settings of the pattern selector on any MKII machine and a succession of ones appears, the memory on that particular setting has not been loaded with a workable program or has lost the one it had. It just goes to show, however, that the memory is never empty of numbers (MKII).

Before programming the MKII model:

a) switch the machine on and press the RR button. Always press the RR button on the completion of every pattern and NEVER switch the machine off and remove the card unless the RR button has been pressed.

b) switch the machine off and feed in the mylar sheet. If this is a little difficult at first, tip in one corner and then straighten the sheet as the turning cogs get a hold.

c) program as usual with the carriage outside the orange marks. If the carriage is not correctly placed, THEN NO SELECTION WILL BE MADE ON THIS MACHINE.

The Three Memories.

Greater memory power means that you can program one after

the other, at the beginning of a piece, three different sets of data for three different patterns, if you wish, on the three positions of the pattern selector - top, middle and bottom.

NB. ONE pattern or program per ONE position. Here are a few examples.

1) The two fishes: three different programs

Because each of the patterns begins from row 1 there is no need to press the RR button when the card returns (see the explanations given earlier). At the beginning of the appropriate row, put the pattern selector to the next position. Knit across for the last row of the previous pattern, and the first row of the new pattern will be selected. Here are the three programs I used on the swatch in the photograph. The three were entered one after the other as soon as I had cast on.

Program 1 Pattern selector, lowest position for overall patterning. Setups as on p.41 in the manual.

Program 2 Pattern selector, highest position for single motif across the whole width. Button 1 up.

```
    150             A motif - Y100,G20 (FNP),G100
1        36
    121
```

Program 3 Pattern selector, middle position, A & B motif, little fish, repeatable mirror image, as previously explained, button 2 up.

```
    142             A motif - Y100,Y1 (FNP),G100
21       60                   B motif - 21 - 60
    121             B motif - Y100,G34 (FNP), G100
```

2) Three consecutive overall patterns

We know that we can use the top position of the pattern selector for overall patterning providing we choose the FNP and the needles marking the pattern limits. The middle position can also be used in the same way on all 910 models. Use the same motif for A & B, and program one in the yellow and the other in the green part of the bed, with the appropriate needle space between. This means therefore, that three overall patterns can be programmed at the onset of knitting on the MKII model. When one program is complete, and there are three different ones, it is necessary to press the RR button. Card returns to the set line. Put the pattern selector to the next position, and press CF.

Three Memories: Two Fishes 910 MKII

This facility will be particularly useful when one is doing traditional Fair Isle, as on yokes, when one needs to change to a different pattern every few rows. The same pattern can be programmed in three different positions. In that case, there is no need to press the RR button when one pattern is complete (see p.51)

3) Offset Patterns

Turn to the lace pattern, heart and treble discs. Copy the top pattern for faggot lace mesh on the Brother onto a mylar card. You will need to enter two programs at the onset of knitting.

Program A - pattern selector, lowest position. Pattern will centre on G1, with the heart to the left, and the discs to the right of 0.

Program B - pattern selector at the top, Y100, G1 (FNP), G100.

The heart pattern will begin at G1 at the right of 0, and the discs will be at the left. Having the extra memory certainly speeds up the pattern change and it saves having to copy out the pattern in the offset position. You merely flip the pattern selector button from bottom to top, or vice-versa to offset the pattern, when the card returns to repeat the sequence.

4) Skirt Patterns

As knitters experiment more boldly with sideways knitted skirts, and the markings for their shaping on the 910 mylar sheet, it will be obvious that the 3 memory facility will be a great advantage. An overall lace, weave or F.I, pattern can be entered on the top or bottom position of the selector for the straight row section between shaped gores, while the program for the latter goes into the machine when the switch is on the middle position.

5) Filet lace - superimposition

Turn back to this section and program the overall lace mesh on the top setting of the pattern selector, and the filet lace hearts and mesh on the middle, before you begin to knit.

NOTE: MKII IS THE TERM I HAVE ADOPTED TO DIFFERENTIATE THIS MODEL FROM ITS PREDECESSOR.

FACILITIES IN COMMON - 910, 500-560.

All three machines have an adjustable pattern repeat system up to sixty stitches wide, marked in a similar way on the card. The machines will knit stocking stitch, Fair Isle, tuck slip-skip (part), weave and (all except the 500) make transfer lace. They will knit overall or selective patterns (motifs or panels).

B = Brother 910. K = Knitmaster 500-560.

1) Pattern begins left of centre.
B Pattern selector up. Pattern begins from Y1 to left.
K N.1.C. centre. No.2 button LH light.

2) Pattern begins right of centre.
B Pattern selector up. Pattern begins from G1 to right.
K N.1.C. centre. No.2 button RH light.

3) Pattern centres at 0 on the bed.
B Pattern selector and all buttons down.
K N.1.C. placed half a pattern width L or R of 0.

4) Pattern same on purl side as on card.
B Pattern selector and all buttons down.
K N.1.C. for pattern. No.2 button RH light.

5) Pattern same on knit side as on card
B Pattern selector down. No.1 button up.
K N.1.C. for pattern. No.2 button LH light.

6) Reverse selection for slip and tuck.
B Pattern selector, choice of positions. No.6 button up.
K N.1.C. for pattern. No.1 button RH light. No.2 button, choice of positions.

7) Reverse for Col.1 & Col.2.(FI).
B As above. Also for 820 Col. changer.
K As above.

8) Vertical expansion.
B Pattern selector, choice of positions. Button 4 up. Elongation at either side.
K N.1.C. as pattern. Button 3 down. Elongation from right.

9) Horizontal expansion.
B Pattern selector, choice of positions. Button 3 up.
K N.1.C. as pattern. Button 4 down.

10) Mirror Image (single pair)
B Pattern selector middle. A & B motif. Button 1 or 2 up. Plot space on needlebed.
K N.1.C. focus. Automatic placing. Button 5 down. Free style with one or two sets of PCs and one or two N.1.Cs. Choice of lights on button two.

11) Mirror Image Repeats.
B As above. Plot space on needlebed and on card. Width of motif up to 29sts.
K As above. Spaces can be varied between 2 sets of PCs, if desired. Width of motif up to 59sts.

12) Single Motif.
B Pattern selector up. Plot space on needlebed. No need to have space on the card.
K Arrange PCs and N.1.C. within chosen space.

13) Jacquard.
B Button 7. Choice of elongation.
K Button 6. No elongation. If required, mark for double length on the card.

14) Upside Down Patterns
B No.5 button up. MKI, enter top row No. Press CF. Repeat & re-program No. for continuous pattern p.51. MKII, continuous pattern automatic. Put up button 5 BEFORE pressing CF p.108.
K Third method of card return p.18. Pattern automatic & continuous.

15) Vertical Reflection
B No.5 button up. MKI, press CF. Pattern automatic and continuous (normal, then upside down). MKII, put up No.5 button AFTER CF for one complete pattern. Put switch up & down for continuous pattern p.108.
K The second method of card return. Card 1(1).p.18. Pattern automatic and continuous.
NB. Top row knitted only ONCE on B & K.

16) Notes on the Memory Systems.
B The machine memorises and holds the pattern on MKI until the batteries expire and 888 flashes in the panel, and on MKII for at least three weeks. When the memory has gone, a series of 1s appear in the panel when M is pressed (MKII). A previous pattern is erased when new numbers are entered.
K The machine loses all memory when it is switched off. During normal operation (current on) THE CARRIAGE MEMORISES THE PCs AND N.1.C. AND THE MACHINE MEMORISES THE PATTERN.p.102 Operation Manual.
The inspection button is put on when you wish to change the pattern width, the pattern card, or move to another line of pattern. Use it also when you want to change lights on

button 2, and have two sets of PCs, two sets of N.1.Cs and button 5 in operation. As soon as the inspection button is put off, the pattern is memorised.

The buttons on the pattern panel can normally be pressed when the carriage is stationary at the end of a row. The pattern modifications will take place on the next row.

BOOK LIST

KNITMASTER 500- 560.

Design with Knit - Regine Faust
A Second Resource Book for Machine Knitters - (section on the SK 500) - Kathleen Kinder

BROTHER 910.

Garment Shaping Electronically - Sara Brooks
Software for Electronic Knitting - Sara Brooks
Diagonal Variation Programs on the KH910 - Shirley Gaskin

CASSETTE TAPES

Knitmaster - 500 - 560 Two instruction tapes for each machine from dealers.

Brother 910 - Two tapes, standard and advanced, from Diane Bennett, 78, Tudor Drive, Yateley, Camberley, Surrey, GU17 7DF.

Notes on brand names

The Silver-Reed machines from Japan are sold by:
Knitmaster U.K.
Singer - Australia
Canada
New Zealand
Studio U.S.A.

The Knitradar is known as the Knit Contour in the U.S.A. Brother machines are sold by Jones + Brother in the U.K. Knitking (U.S.A.) also sell Brother machines under the Knitking label.

INDEX

Embedded Commands: Brother 910 MKII.

These commands have been kindly sent from overseas, only just in time for the book. I have tested them and suggested some knitting applications.

1. To repeat a line of pattern. (alternative method on p. 35)

Enter 880. Press M. The number of the row you are about to knit, as per L window, appears in the purple panel. The card will not move on and the buttons will not function. Switch the machine off and on again to resume normal pattern.

2. To choose the FNP for an allover pattern. Pattern selector down ("always", Note 2 p.34 does not apply).

Press M button. Red light on over pattern selector switch. Enter 999. Press M. Enter 4 positions of pattern. Then enter FNP, which is the only light to appear on the bottom left representation. If you don't enter a new FNP, the machine will show you the FNP for the pattern centred on G1.

To clear: press M. Enter 990 and then M.

3. Test Patterns (without card).

a. Ready light on. Enter 887. Press M. KCI. The fig.1 appears in the window. 1 x 1 needle selection is made beginning at G1. The pattern alternates between G1 & G2 every second row. This is a particularly useful pattern to have for tucks and rib tucks (4rs in pattern). This is the same pattern as Knitmaster 1(5).

b. Press M.(2nd time). The fig.2 appears in the window. On row 1 the needles are selected in groups of 5 beginning at G1. Every 2nd row, the selected groups move one needle place to the right until the sequence is complete (for a broad diagonal stripe in F.I.).

c. Press M (3rd time). The fig.3 appears in the window. On row 1, every 16th needle is selected beginning at Y 4. The pattern moves across one needle space to the right every second row (for a thin diagonal stripe in F.I.).

d. Press M (4th time). The fig.4 appears in the window.

Row 1. Selects G1 and every foll. 5th needle to right and left (2rs).

Row 3. Selects G1 & adjacent needle. Selects in pairs across bed with 3ns at B in between.

Row 5. Selects G1 & 2 adjacent needles. Selects in 3s across the bed with 2ns at B in between.

Row 7. Selects G1 and 3 adjacent needles. Selects in 4s across the bed with one needle in between.

Row 9. Selects all needles.

Row 11. As row 1 and repeat.

A right-angled triangle, standing on its apex, is in the pattern colour.

N.B. The buttons cannot be used on the test patterns, so you are not allowed to make a mistake! The test patterns can be repeated out of sequence ad infinitum. Press the M button until the number you want appears(1 - 4).

To clear. Switch the machine off and on again.

4. To empty the machine completely of memory.

Ready light on. Enter 888. Press M. Ready light goes out, then on. Turn the machine off, then on. Run through M, and 1 appears in the panel.

Special note on No.5 switch (reflection).

The function of this button has been slightly altered. Providing the No.5 switch is put up before the CF is pushed, the pattern will begin from the top line, and the card shoots back there on completion. A short beep signals the beginning and end of a sequence. This means that repeats of an upside-down pattern can be knitted automatically and continuously. This is especially useful for knitting the second sleeve in a sideways knitted top, or for knitting a sleeve downwards from the shoulder. (cf Knitmaster No.3 method of card return)

For upside down lace, choose simple or fine lace patterns, No.1 button up. Change the positions of the carriages. The 820 colour changer can be used.

How then do we knit the patterns from the lace diagonal p.65 and the quarter Shetland Star p.74?

Answer 1: Press CF. Card goes to r1 of pattern. NOW PUT UP NO.5 BUTTON. This will produce one complete star or one complete diamond (also for mitts & socks p.91).

To alternate the direction of the card: move the No.5 switch up and down during the knitting, so that you can knit the tessellated Shetland Star and repeats of the lace diamond.

Order a. When the card is going down as per normal, put No.5 switch up.

b. When the card is going up for an upside-down pattern, put the No.5 switch down, and this, incidentally, is how you cancel the upside-down reading. The card resumes its normal run on the next sequence.

Answer 2: Once you have used the embedded commands 999 (see 2,p.107) to change or check the FNP, and 990 to clear it, you will find you have changed the function of button 5.

999 - for automatic upside-down patterns.

990 - for automatic reflection (as MKI).

THE ELECTRONIC GARTER CARRIAGE (Brother). This accessory should be available early 1985. Information & comment will, I hope, be in my Ribber Bk.Vol.2.